ONLY THE GOOD DIE YOUNG

D1466645

ONLY THE GOOD DIE YOUNG

The Rock 'n' Roll Book of the Dead

ROBERT DUNCAN

Harmony Books/ New York

Published by Harmony Books,
a division of Crown Publishers, Inc.
225 Park Avenue South, New York,
New York 10003

HARMONY and colophon are trademarks of
Crown Publishers, Inc.
Manufactured in the United States of America

**Library of Congress
Cataloging-in-Publication Data**
Duncan, Robert.
  Only the good die young.
  Includes index.
  1. Rock musicians—United States—
Biography. 2. Singers—United States—
Biography. I. Title.
ML400.D85   1986   784.5′4′00922 [B]
84-27970
ISBN 0-517-55757-6

10 9 8 7 6 5 4 3 2 1
First Edition

TO GEORGE NORTON STONE

Thanks to Laura Palmer and Cloverdale; my agent, Barbara
Lowenstein; my patient editor, Doug Abrams; and Jim and Danielle
Sotet. And R.H. And J.R.

CONTENTS

1 PROLOGUE: The End 1

2 HANK WILLIAMS: The Original 3

3 JOHNNY ACE: The Games People Play 11

4 BUDDY HOLLY: Angel Without Wings 17

5 SAM COOKE: Saints and Sinners 21

6 OTIS REDDING: Fire on Ice 27

7 BRIAN JONES: No Satisfaction 33

8 JIMI HENDRIX: Up from the Skies 45

9 JIM MORRISON: The End as Prologue 59

10 JANIS JOPLIN: American Crosses 77

11 GRAM PARSONS: The Lord's Burning Rain 91

12   DUANE ALLMAN and BERRY OAKLEY:
Free Birds 101

13   RONNIE VAN ZANT and
LYNYRD SKYNYRD: More Free Birds 107

14   SID VICIOUS: No Future 111

15   KEITH MOON: Happy Jack Was a Man 119

16   JOHN BELUSHI: Blue Brother 129

17   BOB MARLEY: Exodus 143

18   KAREN CARPENTER: No More Songs About
Buildings and Food 155

19   ELVIS PRESLEY: Rust Never Sleeps 159

20   JOHN LENNON: The King Is Gone 169

21   EPILOGUE: The Future as Epitaph 173

22   ROCK 'N' ROLL HEAVEN 175

SOURCE NOTES 179

INDEX 187

ONLY THE GOOD DIE YOUNG

PROLOGUE
The End

*T*he End.

What a nice place to start a book. It takes the pressure off. But what better place to start a book about the dead.

Ah, the dead.

And I'm not talking about Jerry, Bobby, Phil, et al. These aren't the Dead who drop acid and always play too long. And by and large these dead aren't very grateful. I'm talking about rot and ruination. I'm talking about *finis,* over and *out.* I'm talking about the dead who have reached the *end.*

Which brings up Morrison, of course.

In 1971 Jim Morrison was about as close to the end as a man can get without actually checking out. Jim Morrison, in fact, was about as close to the end as the composer of "The End" could ever want to be. He was as brilliantly close to the end as his idol, the French poet Rimbaud, had once been. Jim Morrison was eating opium and writing poetry in Paris and had stipulated in his will that he be buried near Rimbaud in the artists' cemetery, Père-Lachaise, and Jim Morrison was close to the end—but on top of the world. He was so on top of the world that he even began to think he was close to a beginning.

Jim Morrison was one smart cookie.

Jim Morrison *was* close to a beginning, a rebirth. And it was to be a rebirth so massive and spectacular that you might almost think he planned it—and, of course, there are some who think he did. There are also some who think he's alive and enjoying the fruits of his rebirth. And there is even one of those who thinks he knows it firsthand—he says he *is* Morrison and turns up periodically to promote his autobiography, the title of which has something to do with a mythical "Bank of Louisiana." But it's very likely that Morrison is neither alive nor writing about banks.

The likelihood is that, like so many young romantics before him, Jim Morrison is very unoriginally, very uncleverly dead and that, finally, the only thing he really planned was for a pit in Père-Lachaise to contain his mortal stench.

That not all of the dead have reached the end, that in a sense some are not entirely dead, must truly be the moral of the Jim Morrison story. It is also, more or less, what this book is about: those who live on in death. This book is about myths and mythmaking in rock 'n' roll, the music that begat a culture.

It's about some rock 'n' rollers who, by the very act of reaching the end, started out.

It's about, on the one hand, Jim Morrison, a bloated, over-weight, heroin-addicted, lonely, expatriate, twenty-seven-year-old singer and songwriter with desperate pretensions to being a serious poet but who in 1971 was about as far from literary Parnassus as he was from the pop Parnassus he had once occupied and which he now disdained.

It's about, on the one hand, Jim Morrison, who liked to think he lived bravely, for all to admire, out there on the edge of the end, but who in 1971 was mostly just washed up—and then dead.

It's about Jim Morrison, who became much bigger in death than he ever was in life, and for whom death, to paraphrase Ian Hunter, was indeed a Santa Claus.

On the other hand, it's about Buddy Holly, who never did nothing his mama couldn't be proud of and died—at twenty-one, on top of the charts and destined for even bigger things—because he wanted to get to the next town early enough to do his laundry.

It's about Buddy Holly: cut short for the cleaning.

And it's about poor, damned Sid Vicious, for whom dead was merely a birthright.

It's about rock's attraction to death and death's attraction to rock. And, as much as rock 'n' roll is a reflection of our collective dream, it's about the way we all live—and die.

2
HANK WILLIAMS

The Original

Down the road from the Hank Williams Museum, on the road that goes from Memphis through the Mississippi Delta, the middle-aged white man who owns the largest oldies store in New Orleans told me that he invented rock 'n' roll.

"I'm walking back and forth, jumping up and down backstage, and I'm screaming and hollering. 'Where the hell is he? Where the hell is that son of a bitch?'" said the middle-aged white man who claimed he had invented rock 'n' roll. He was screaming and hollering again, right there in the middle of his record store.

Customers engrossed in his unparalleled collection of oldies either didn't notice or pretended not to notice—or maybe they'd gotten used to it: The middle-aged white man had been carrying on in this fashion for thirty years.

He continued ranting. "I've got a goddamn show to do! A goddamn New Year's *Eve* show to do! And I've got hundreds, no thousands, *thousands* of people out there waiting, and where do you think that son of a bitch was? I'll tell ya where he was. He was lying in the back of a powder-blue Cadillac down there south of Canton, Ohio. He was dead, son of a bitch. Pills and booze. Dead, I tell ya. Dead—you seen it in the movie. But you didn't see me, did ya? Tearin' my hair out backstage. Dead, the son of a bitch. Dead. That's all she wrote. The end."

But of course it was only the beginning. Hank Williams was indeed the original dead rock star; the year was 1953, and rock 'n' roll hadn't even been invented.

Hank Williams was a great artist—singer and songwriter—in his own right. At the same time he was a bridge—*the* bridge, perhaps—between country & western and rockabilly. This sound, combined with black gospel music, produced rock 'n' roll. But ultimately the myth, the legend, of Hank Williams depends as much on his decadent way of life as on his art. "A poet of limits, fear, and failure," the critic Greil Marcus once termed him. And somehow Williams's death signifies that he meant it, that he wasn't just faking. And he wasn't.

Jailed after a drinking jag in Alexander City, Alabama, just four months before his death, Williams was philosophical, gaunt, unshaven, and unshirted. He stood before his jail-cell door, at once twisting away from the flashing cameras and snarling at them like some cornered, but clearly cowed, junkyard dog. He was a bag of bones staring out through terrified eyes—a refugee. In a white five-gallon cowboy hat.

Recalling a typical evening on the road with Hank Williams, his sometime touring associate Minnie Pearl described this scene to Hank, Jr.: "As I walked backstage, they were bringing Hank up the steps. He looked at me. I sound overdramatic when I tell it, but it was true—the look that he had on his face was of such pleading that I just never will forget it. He said, 'Minnie, I just can't work. Tell them I can't work!'

"He sang maybe a couple of songs, then the promoter told me to stay with him between shows. He said, 'Minnie, he may listen to you.'

"This was between shows in San Diego, and we were drinking around, trying to keep him from getting anything that would make him get in worse shape than he was. So we started singing. I remember his feet were big and his legs were so long, and he hunkered down in the car with his feet up, and he was looking out the side of the car, and he was singing 'I Saw the Light.' And then he stopped, and he turned around, and his face broke up, and he said, 'Minnie, I don't see no more light.'

"At that time, Hank's life was a tunnel, the way he described it. And if he could have seen one ray of light come in, we might have saved him."

The legend has it that he got into that tunnel via pills and booze, tons of pills and booze. One version of the story says that the whole thing started with a chronic back problem that led—not surprisingly, in those days of laissez-faire pharmacology—to a chronic painkiller problem. But, considering his taste for the grape, it's hard to imagine that his involvement with pharmaceuticals was entirely inadvertent. In fact, as Michael Bane observed: "[Hank] provided a prototype for the hard-living, hard-drinking, got-no-future-but-I'm-sure-as-hell-on-my-way hillbilly singer, and that prototype launched a thousand singers who wanted to do it 'just like Ole Hank done it.' . . . There's this nagging feeling in Nashville, even today, that, well, so what if he *died* doing it, Hank's route is still the only way to go."

But like so many who follow that route, Hank Williams had hellhounds on his trail. He was a refugee from his own dark soul.

Born Hiram Williams in a two-room shack in Mount Olive, Alabama, on September 17, 1923, son of a sharecropper and sometime train engineer ("Hear that lonesome whistle blow . . . ") and a mother who played gospel piano, he was the epitome of southern poor white trash. Claiming to be suffering from a lingering shell shock incurred in the First World War, his father abandoned the family when Hank was only seven to commit himself to a veteran's hospital. But shell shock was surely just the old man's way of getting around admitting his alcoholism and of being allowed to malinger his life away at the taxpayers' expense, like the true Snopes that he was. Young Hank, his sister, Lycrecia, and their Baptist, God-fearing mama, Lilly, were left to their own devices.

For a while, Mama eked them out a living playing her piano in their friendly local Baptist church, where young Hank Williams, like so many other of our pop geniuses, learned his music—in the choir. Mama also took $3.50 of her scarce, hard-earned money and bought Hank a guitar. Mama gave him his music.

The relatives who took them all in when Mama could no

longer cope alone were itinerant rail workers, like his daddy had been. They worked hard, lived poor, and didn't have much time to supervise a precocious eleven-year-old. Young Hank found he enjoyed hanging around at the Saturday-night dances learning a different kind of music from what his mama played in church. It was secular music—crazy, happy, and frankly, devilish country & western music. It was about another kind of ecstasy: moonshine whiskey. Of course, what Hank Williams had found at those Saturday hoedowns—country picking and country drinking—was exactly what he would devote the rest of his life to. All 18 years of it.

Perhaps his adoring mama sensed the new course her son's life was taking, but the following year she took Hank and his sister to Montgomery, where she opened a rooming house. In Montgomery, Alabama, another critical element of Hank's musical education came together when he met an older black man named Rufus Payne, better known around the Montgomery streets that were his stage as "Tee-Tot." Selling peanuts, shining shoes, and most important, singing and playing on the streets with his black friend, the little white-trash boy learned an invaluable lesson. "Tee-Tot," says Hank Williams, Jr., "taught Daddy to sing the blues, not just mimic a black man, but to reach out and touch that common pool of emotion."

Hank Williams was still only twelve years old when he first reached out and touched that common emotional pool, taking first prize—and the handsome sum of $15—in an amateur-night contest in Montgomery by singing a tune called "The WPA Blues." Soon, temporarily dubbed the Singing Kid, he had his twice-a-week radio show on Montgomery's WSFA. By the time he was fifteen, he had a backup band, the soon-to-be-famous Drifting Cowboys, and a manager, mother Lilly Williams, and he was playing every honky-tonk they could get him into between Tennessee and southern 'Bama. But he was still basically going nowhere. And then in Banks, Alabama, he met Audrey Mae Sheppard, the second strong woman in his life.

Hank and Audrey Mae married in December 1944, and within two years she had horned in on a Ping-Pong game at the studio of

WSM, radio home of the Grand Ole Opry, in Nashville and gotten Fred and Wesley Rose, cofounders of country music's most influential song-publishing house, to agree to have a listen to a few of Hank Williams's tunes. One of the six songs Hank played that day was "Six More Miles to the Graveyard." Fred Rose would hone the young man's songwriting technique and get him a recording contract with MGM and build him a career. For Hank, it was the first mile on the road to the top, but it was also the first mile of a short road down. In any event, with Audrey Mae pushing, the race was definitely on.

In the summer of 1948, Hank made it onto country music's top radio farm team, becoming a regular on the "Louisiana Hayride" show out of Shreveport, and his records began to climb the country charts. In 1949 "Lovesick Blues" hit number one. And on June 11, 1949, Hank Williams finally achieved the summit of country & western success, striding onstage at Nashville's Ryman Auditorium and into WSM's "Grand Ole Opry" program, the "Ed Sullivan Show" of its place and time. "Imagine Elvis on stage, or the Beatles in their first American tour," says Hank, Jr. Hank Williams walked off the Ryman stage that evening after six encores and instantly, automatically, became the biggest name in country music.

With songs like "Hey, Good Lookin'," "Cold Cold Heart," "Honky Tonkin'," "Kaw-Liga," "Your Cheatin' Heart," and "Jambalaya," he would not only continue to occupy the country summit, but make it all his own. Ultimately his musical influence would be heard throughout popular music, including in the music of Elvis and the Beatles, which he would not live to hear. And yet, as Greil Marcus had said, "Williams sang for a community to which he could not belong; he sang to a God in whom he could not quite believe. . . ." For all his fame and fortune Hank remained that spiritual refugee.

"There were demons in my father," speculates Hank, Jr., "and because of the way he was, or the people around him, or the temper of the times, they were demons he could never exorcise. He was practically an alcoholic by the time he was fifteen— necessary to survive the clubs he played, I think. Nowadays we call those places 'toilets.' . . . He'd hurt his back early on, and the pain nagged at him for as long as he was alive. Sometimes he was able to drown it in liquor, and later he found an easing in the pills. Or maybe he found an excuse for the liquor and the pills in his pain. Who's to say?"

Hank, Jr., continues: "Daddy was haunted by his genius, and when the blues came around at midnight he had no place to turn, no one to grab ahold of. . . .

"The problem was (I think) that despite the hangers-on, well-wishers, managers, wife, and what have you, nobody ever gave the slightest thought to helping Daddy cope with his success. He was successful beyond his wildest imagination. Literally beyond his wildest imagination, and he couldn't imagine what to do next."

Hank, Sr., did what so many of his haunted brethren have done: He headed further and further down that tunnel of pills and booze. In 1952, "Jambalaya" hit number one. The same year he was fired from the Grand Ole Opry for being constantly drunk and was divorced by Audrey Mae. He begged her to take him back until the final decree.

In 1952, Hank Williams was completing the blueprint for the rock 'n' roll lifestyle. He was at the height of his commercial and artistic success, but he was hell-bent on abusing his body to the limit. By the end of the year, he had pushed himself over the edge.

Some DJ in Canton, Ohio, had offered Hank very good money to play a New Year's Day gig, and despite an unusual near-blizzard the morning of January 1, Hank Williams managed to get himself out of the house early and on the road heading north. Perhaps he thought about turning over a new leaf. Hank, Jr.: "Daddy had hired a driver named Charles Carr to drive him to Canton and had talked him into stopping along the way for Daddy to get a shot of painkiller for his back. Carr began to worry that Hank was lying so quietly, and in Oak Hill, West Virginia, he stopped to check."

Wrong leaf.

Hank Williams was dead at the age of twenty-nine in the back seat of a powder-blue Cadillac on his way to a gig in Canton, Ohio—and his "Take These Chains from My Heart" promptly shot to number one on the nation's country & western charts.

"They came to Montgomery by the tens of thousands—some say by the hundreds of thousands—when they buried Daddy," writes Hank Williams, Jr., "and no one could remember such an outpouring of grief for any one person in the South since the end of the Civil War. Hank was dead. No last names were necessary." Hank was buried in the Oakwood Cemetery Annex. Hank Williams Jr., continues: "To get to my father's grave, you go down a road with seven bridges, and someone wrote a song about that [Steve Young's "Seven Bridges Road," later covered by the Eagles]. . . .

"There were songs about Hank in heaven, meeting Hank in the by-and-by, Hank's ghost, Hank's soul—Hank dead was bigger than Hank alive. Hank alive was just a hillbilly singer—Hank dead was a myth, the Legend of Hank Williams." The coroner ruled heart failure. Hank's heart just couldn't take any more drinking. His son continues. "His biggest song of 1953 was 'I'll Never Get Out of This World Alive.'"

(And if you doubt for a moment the influence of the myth of Hank Williams on future generations of rock, as well as country, stars, think back to the famous line of Jim Morrison's, later the title of his best-selling—and mythmaking—biography: "No one here gets out alive.")

3
JOHNNY ACE

The Games People Play

The singers and musicians I grew up with transcend nostalgia—Buddy Holly and Johnny Ace are just as valid to me today as then.

—Bob Dylan

*Y*ou can't do a book about dead rock stars and not mention Johnny Ace.

Yes indeed, Johnny Ace remains valid—but maybe not in the way Bob Dylan thinks. Most people who have heard the name Johnny Ace would be hard pressed to come up with any song titles. He had his first big R & B hit in 1953 with a tune called "My Song"—not to be confused with "Your Song" by Elton John. He was in the navy during World War II. He started out in music playing piano in a band led by a man named Adolph Duncan. He often hung out around Beale Street, the black main street and birthplace of the blues, in his hometown of Memphis, Tennessee, jamming with B. B. King and Bobby "Blue" Bland, from whom he may have learned some of his vocal technique. A mellow baritone who

featured himself in mellow arrangements, a sort of black Perry Como, he has also been compared to Nat "King" Cole. His second and biggest hit was called "Pledging My Love." It was released in 1955, but by then Johnny Ace was already long in the grave.

Which brings us to what everybody remembers Johnny Ace for. No one really knows what happened that night, but maybe it went something like this:

It was Christmas Eve, 1954, and it was Houston—a long way from the North Pole. But Johnny Ace knew that Santa don't come to black folks, not even if they're living next door. For Johnny Ace, Christmas was just another night out on the long, never-ending road. He was not worried how Santa was gonna find his way to Houston; he was worried about how Johnny Ace was gonna find his way back to Memphis. Johnny Ace was sitting in front of a folding card table in the steamy backstage area at Houston's cavernous City Auditorium. He took a pull on the pint of Southern Comfort that traditionally rested in the right-hand inside pocket of his expensive Italian silk suit. Then he took his little pearl-handled Colt .32 from his left inside pocket, put it on the table, and spun it around. Between the seven bands, the promoter, and all the promoter's various secretaries, girlfriends, and ex-wives, there must have been close to a hundred people crowded into the four or five rooms, three broom closets, and two bathrooms. The door to the men's room flew open and out stumbled half of Johnny Ace's band enveloped in a cloud of marijuana smoke. There was one down and two or three more shows left to do that night, and then it would be on to Baton Rouge, for three or four shows more. And on and on.

"Say!" Johnny called out to his band through the haze. "What do you got says I can?" He spun the chamber on the Colt, held it to his temple, and grinned. "What do you got, fellas?"

One of the band members, Slugger, stopped dead in his tracks, his jaw dropping. The horn section stumbled into him and each groggily raised his eyes. Johnny cocked the revolver.

"Oh, shit!" said the new trumpet player, looking away, freaked.

"C'mon," said Johnny, "who's in?"

Recovering himself, Slugger stared Johnny in the eye and pulled a wad from his shiny black pocket. "Shit," said the bass player, who'd been with Johnny Ace a long time and had seen this part of the act before, "I'll take that shit. You got change for a Ben Franklin, Johnny Ace, or do I have to lay out a whole month's pay on one shitty-ass Johnny Ace joke."

"I'll call ya," said Johnny, unfolding his own hundred-dollar bill from a snakeskin billfold and laying it on the table next to the bass player's. "Don't be shy with your money on my account, Slugger."

Johnny had pulled this Russian roulette stunt once before, the bassist recalled. It was in Shreveport—or was in Kingsport? Anyway, some raggedy-ass Dixie town. They all liked to play poker. Except for Johnny. Johnny liked to gamble, but mostly he did it with other folks' women and his own fast car. That's why he packed that piece, 'cause when you gamble with other folks' women in that part of the world, you gamble with your life.

But Slugger remembered that other time when Johnny had pulled out his revolver and tried to up the ante. He had been bored with the women and the cars and the Southern Comfort and the adulation of thousands in the dark. He had needed a new thrill. So he had laid his money down, and the band, thinking he was joking, had laid their money down, and there had been this long pause. And finally Johnny had looked up at them and smiled and said, "I oughta just *take* your damn money for you being such a dumb buncha niggers thinkin' I'd do somethin' so stupid to a sweet young thing like me." And then he had gotten up and walked away from the hundred. The band had won the bet.

But that had been Kingsport—or Shreveport. The fateful night was Houston, and the rest of the band just walked away. "Shit," they said.

"Shee-it," said Slugger. "All right, Johnny Ace, I'll play. I'll take your hundred bucks. C'mon, Johnny Ace, let's play."

It was so steamy and smoky and drunken loud backstage on Christmas Eve, 1954, at the Houston City Auditorium that the report of a Colt .32 *almost* went unnoticed. It did take a minute.

Suddenly, one of the promoter's girlfriends screamed, and every-one hit the floor. Everyone, that is, except Slugger, who stood frozen beside a card table with a piece of Johnny Ace's brain on his hand. This time the band lost the bet. But then so had Johnny Ace.

He wasn't going to be around to collect his money. And he wasn't going to be around to collect his "fame." Because the only thing that established a place for Johnny Ace in rock history was the way he died—blowing his brains out backstage playing Russian roulette.

It makes a great story.

4
BUDDY HOLLY

Angel Without Wings

*U*nlike Johnny Ace, Buddy Holly is not best remembered for his death. Actually, what makes Buddy Holly so interesting is his music, which remains fresh 25 years later.

Bob Dylan thinks Buddy Holly transcends nostalgia. Paul McCartney agrees with Dylan so thoroughly that he purchased the rights to the entire Buddy Holly catalog. The rock group that gave Crosby and Stills their Nash felt likewise and so called themselves the Hollies. And though there are cultists who believe that, like Jim Morrison, he faked his death and now lives incognito in New Mexico, Buddy Holly's untimely demise is not what makes him so interesting to so many in rock 'n' roll. But it doesn't hurt.

Buddy Holly was a good guy. A decent guy. Even a clean-cut all-American guy. Indeed, if some rock deaths certify the deceased as a demon (Jim Morrison, Brian Jones), his certified him as the angel he always sounded like and in one sense—and certainly compared to his rock 'n' roll peers—was. One of his high school teachers practically beatified him when she said after his death: "He was a quiet kid—wasn't any great student, but didn't cause any trouble either, you understand." Buddy Holly was dedicated to music, which in his era (as in ours) just happened to be dominated by rock 'n' roll. And Buddy Holly died in that horrible plane crash because Buddy Holly wanted to take his music wherever it would go. Even to Clear Lake, Iowa.

A lot of rock stars die from heroin. And from driving very fast while under the influence of alcohol. And assorted other hazards of what the Eagles (some of whom should know) have called "life in the fast lane." Not Buddy Holly. Buddy Holly, in fact, is one of the few rock 'n' roll stars to actually die accidentally on the job.

He was born Charles Hardin Holley in Lubbock, Texas, on September 7, 1938 (a slick manager had the million-dollar idea that in an era when everyone changed their name Buddy should change his by dropping the *e*). Buddy didn't ever know much about show biz. What he knew about was pickin' and singin'. At five he won a $5 prize at a Lubbock amateur show for his rendition of "Down the River of Memories." Before he was a teen, he had a functional knowledge of the guitar, violin, and piano.

In high school, he was influenced by his parents' old 78s of "Singing Brakeman" Jimmie Rodgers, by Hank Williams, who succeeded Rodgers as the King of Country Music, and by Bob Wills, who with his Texas Playboys brought the happy slickness of big-band jazz to cowboy-style country music in a form dubbed Western Swing, much as Buddy would later bring the happy slickness of Tin Pan Alley pop to rock.

Soon, young Charles Hardin Holley formed a group called the Western and Pop Band. The Western and Pop Band had gained enough local fame by 1954 to attract a contract from Decca Records in Nashville. The deal seemed to inspire Buddy to write songs. He wrote "Peggy Sue" and "That'll Be the Day," among a host of others, but his career stalled, and after an almost two-year affiliation, Decca dropped the group.

Back in Lubbock, Buddy and Jerry Allison, the future Crickets, formed an all-purpose local opening act. One day the pair opened for Elvis Presley, and Buddy Holly saw the light. "We owe it all to Elvis," he would later tell an interviewer.

In February 1957, Holly and Allison, joined by Sonny Curtis (later to gain solo fame as writer of "The Mary Tyler Moore Show" theme) on guitar and Don Guess on bass and calling themselves the Crickets, left Lubbock for Clovis, New Mexico, and Norman Petty's studio. The first song they recorded was a rockin' remake of a number previously turned down by Decca. It was called "That'll Be the Day." By the end of 1957, having been picked up by Coral Records, the song was number three on the pop charts. But, once more, it was only the beginning, just the first of eight Buddy Holly songs (some of them released only under the Crickets name) to reach the charts in the following 12 months. Then they took off on a wildly successful tour in which they became the first white rock 'n' roll act to play Harlem's famed Apollo Theatre—the theater's booking agent, hard as it may be to believe now, mistook their pristine, non-gospel sound for that of a black act. During this tour Buddy Holly did not get drunk a lot, take drugs, play Russian roulette, or generally behave in a self-destructive way, but at the end of it Buddy Holly and the Crickets self-destructed.

Buddy left the Crickets and moved to Greenwich Village. He wanted to take his pop-oriented rock in newer, more artistic, more intellectual directions.

In New York, Holly promptly met, proposed to, and married a beautiful young Puerto Rican girl named Maria Elena Santiago. To complete his new Bohemian life, the young rocker also promptly started to go broke. The breakup with the Crickets had tied up his royalties and his ability to release any new recordings. He did do some recording during his Village phase, but finally, with great reluctance, his decision to go artsy forced him to go commercial (for a while, at least, till the legal hassles were cleared), and Buddy Holly hooked up with the Winter Dance Party Tour for a series of one-nighters through the Midwest at its snowiest and coldest. The tour included J. P. Richardson (better known as "the Big Bopper"), then riding high with "Chantilly Lace," and Chicano rocker Ritchie Valens of "C'mon Let's Go" fame. Also in Buddy's backup group was a young Texan bass player named Waylon Jennings.

It was an ultimate rock 'n' roll grind, this Winter Dance Party Tour. But it didn't cause Buddy Holly to take to junk or to recklessness. It did, however, get his clothes a little dirty. And so, on the evening of February 3, 1959, so that he might get his laundry done, clean-cut, all-American Buddy Holly, along with Richardson and Valens, left the boys who continued on by tour bus and chartered a plane to the site of the next night's gig. The broken fuselage of that plane, containing the bodies of Richardson and Holly, was found the next morning in a cornfield near Clear Lake, Iowa. Nearby was the body of Valens, thrown from the craft on impact.

It is still not known whether the late, great Charles Hardin Holley actually had ring around the collar. In any case, it is presumed that when that plane went down on earth, up in heaven, angels sang.

5

SAM COOKE

Saints and Sinners

Sam Cooke was a man who could turn a spiritual into a fucksong for God. More than that, onstage he was the black Jesus. And when the owner of a sleazy Los Angeles motel pumped three bullets into Sam very late one December night, it was truly the Soul Crucifixion.

The *Chicago Defender* described his hometown wake in the Windy City this way:

"Thousands of screaming, crying, pushing people thronged the area surrounding A. R. Leak's Funeral Home . . . in a frantic attempt to see the body of singer Sam Cooke. . . .

"Both chapels, each holding about 300 people, were filled . . . and the urgency of many to get a last look at Sam resulted in near chaos, with young and old being crushed in the process. . . .

"When the plate glass in a front door at Leak's chapel gave way under the pressure of the crowd, Spencer Leak, a son of A. R. Leak, Sr., shouted, 'There are just too many of them.'

"One emotional woman when crushed while attempting to step over the threshold screamed, 'Please let me in. I've never seen anything like this in my life.'

"Cooke's coffin was covered with glass, to the disappointment of many. A blind woman, who came to pay her respects and

perhaps 'touch' her singing idol, was rammed against a door frame and had to be pulled over the entrance by funeral parlor employees."

Including the figures from an earlier wake in Los Angeles, his adopted hometown, an estimated 200,000 mourners filed past the body of Sam Cooke. And around the country, millions more wept. In Memphis, the singer's death was the occasion for the kind of banner headline that the white-owned-and-operated daily, the *Commercial-Appeal,* reserved for heads of state. But there it was: SAM COOKE DEAD.

The year was 1964, the year that gave us the Beatles and Bob Dylan's "Blowin' in the Wind," and the beginning in earnest of the Swinging Sixties. It was the beginning, in fact, of a whole new era, an era that Sam had eagerly anticipated and an era he had helped to create. And when the year that gave us all of that also took him, Sam Cooke was only thirty-one.

Like so much else, most notably the electric blues, that is important to black culture and to American music, Sam Cooke was born in Chicago. For those with sacred calendars, the date to mark is January 22, 1933. Like so many other musicians, he was the son, one of eight, of a Baptist minister. He was handsome and he was holy and, holy shit, could he sing. By the time he was eighteen he was the new lead singer in the Soul Stirrers, arguably the most popular gospel group of its day and a virtual institution in black America since the thirties. Sam had a hard act to follow because he was replacing the revered R. H. Harris, "whose quivering tenor," according to music historian Joe McEwen, "was the forerunner of the modern soul falsetto." But in short order the teenage Sam Cooke had managed to eclipse Harris completely and to claim the title King of the Gospel Mountain. Something about the way he made those spirituals swing.

Six years on the road watching Sam Cooke work his magic on crowds gave Soul Stirrers manager J. W. Alexander a few secular notions. One of them resulted in Alexander taking Sam into a studio in 1956 to record a pop song called "Lovable." And while "Lovable" proved rather forgettable, Sam himself was now bitten by the secular bug. Signing on the now-legendary Robert

"Bumps" Blackwell as producer, Alexander borrowed some
time in the studio of Specialty Records, the Soul Stirrers' label.
Bumps first took Sam's record in 1957 to a garage label called
Keen Records. And, by all commercial logic, that is where Sam
Cooke's pop output should have expired. But the first Sam Cooke
record on Keen happened to be a billowing ballad entitled "You
Send Me," which sold over 1.5 million copies and climbed to
number one on the *Billboard* pop charts.

Two years later, Cooke finished out his Keen contract by
releasing "Wonderful World," his biggest hit since the first, and
on that high note, Blackwell and Alexander took Sam to RCA.
After Allen Klein—later manager of both the Beatles and the
Stones—brought some of his negotiating muscle to bear, RCA
returned to Blackwell, Alexander, Cooke, and Klein a sum
unheard of in the music business in those days. According to
Phillip Norman, "Sam Cooke became . . . the first pop name to
receive a million dollars without singing a note. . . . " He became
the first of the instant superstars of rock—after, of course, eight
years on the road with the Soul Stirrers, 10 singles for Keen, and
a lifetime of honing his music.

RCA executives may have felt a little burned themselves when
the initial release from their million-dollar baby—a teenybop tune
called "Teenage Sonata"—didn't exactly burn up the charts. But
this worry was short-lived. Sam Cooke's next release was the
irresistible "Chain Gang," and it shot to the top of the charts.
"From that point on," says Joe McEwen, "Sam Cooke was
rarely without a Top-40 hit." A partial list includes such sixties
landmarks as "Cupid," "Twistin' the Night Away," "Having a
Party," "Bring It on Home to Me" (backed up by Lou Rawls),
"Another Saturday Night," the original "Little Red Rooster,"
"Shake," and the posthumous "A Change Is Gonna Come,"
Sam's aborted bid to get political, reportedly inspired by Dylan.
But, in addition to being just a wonderful singer, Sam Cooke,
like all the great rock stars (and many of the dead ones), was a
cultural figure.

To young black America, Sam Cooke was as pure and smooth
and gentle as his voice. He was wholesome without being

saccharine—Pat Boone with balls. Just as his friend and partner J. W. Alexander had anticipated, Sam Cooke was the kind of guy that black girls could envision bringing home to meet the folks, the kind that the folks could envision their little angel marrying.

To black America, Sam Cooke was hope. He had risen from relatively modest beginnings to become a millionaire. It wasn't just that he wore silk suits and drove fancy cars: Sam Cooke *used* his money. He built something with it: a management company, a record label (Sar/Derby), and a music publisher. Sam Cooke was savvy and industrious. Sam Cooke wasn't going to die broke like so many other black heroes before him. Sam Cooke was a Good Example.

What happened on South Figueroa Avenue in Los Angeles on the night of December 11, 1964, did not sit well with black America. Some people flatly refused to believe the stories they had read in the white press. Some believed the rumor that Sam Cooke was set up and rubbed out by the Mafia because he'd gotten too independent—and too independently successful—in the allegedly Mafia-dominated music business. As always, some believed he was not dead at all.

The true story was ugly indeed according to the newspaper reports. It began at a Hollywood party where Cooke, thirty-one and married, picked up Lisa Boyer, a twenty-two-year-old of "British-Chinese backgrounds," according to the papers. After offering her a lift home, Boyer reported to police, Sam instead "kidnapped" her and forced her to go to a motel with him, where together they registered as "Mr. and Mrs. Cooke." (To some, the kidnapping story begins to break down at this point. Nevertheless . . .)

According to Boyer's testimony at the inquest, Sam then "dragged me to that room, and I again asked him to take me home. He turned the night latch, pushed me into bed and pinned me down. He kept saying, 'We're just gonna talk.' . . . He pulled my sweater off and ripped my dress. I knew he was going to rape me." Whereupon Sam Cooke promptly went to the bathroom. While he was in there Lisa Boyer made good her escape, taking Sam's clothes with her for insurance.

Boyer testified that Sam, dressed in only a sport coat, quickly gave chase, following her to the motel manager's office, where she went looking for a phone to call for help. But the manager's office was closed, and Boyer managed to slip away unseen to a pay phone on the street. Believing Boyer to be hiding inside, or so the story goes, Cooke began pounding on the manager's door, calling out, "Where's the girl?"

Inside, fifty-five-year-old Bertha Franklin told him to go away and get the police. Finally, Cooke broke the door down and lunged for Franklin, who pushed him aside, drew her .22 pistol, and fired three times.

"Lady, you shot me," said Cooke, according to Franklin's testimony at the inquest. And then, said the motel manager, "He ran at me again. I started fighting with a stick. The first time I hit him it broke."

And so she hit him again. And again. Eventually the police did get there. But the soul singer, like the dreams that so many people had invested in him, was strictly DOA.

6
OTIS REDDING

Fire on Ice

Otis Redding's hero was Sam Cooke, which seems strange. When you think of Otis, the first thing you think of is roughness. You think of his rip-it-up, pedal-to-the-metal version of "Satisfaction"—the one that Jagger himself later copped for the live shows. When you think of Sam, you think smooth all the way: "You Send Me" and "Wonderful World" and all the rest of his famous ballads.

So why did Otis Redding idolize Sam Cooke, when their styles were seemingly so different? Because Otis was not just rough. He was an accomplished ballad singer, too. "Try a Little Tenderness," "I've Been Loving You Too Long," "These Arms of Mine," and "My Lover's Prayer" were all ballads. And "Dock of the Bay," the song that finally put Otis Redding over the top with white America, was a ballad, too.

But ballads weren't the only thing that Sam and Otis had in common. Like his hero, Otis Redding was picked off in his prime. Dead.

In a lot of ways, Otis was the nice guy that Sam only pretended to be. Says co-writer and band leader Steve Cropper: "My original feeling for Otis wound up to be my final feeling: He was a pure man. His love for people showed up in his songs. He was always trying to get back to his baby—or he missed her, she was the greatest thing in the world. His approach was always *positive*.

"I first met him in 1962. At the time, Otis was sort of a road manager, singer, and driver for Johnny Jenkins and the Pinetoppers. They'd come up to Memphis to cut a bunch of sides, and Otis was just sitting in a corner of the studio all day long, and every once in a while he'd get up and say, 'Man, I sure would like to cut a song!' So after we'd finished cutting Jenkins, there was forty minutes left, and we said, 'OK, let's see what this guy's got.'"

The version of the story told by Stax Records' chief Jim Stewart presents an even humbler Otis and an even more unlikely, but nonetheless true, discovery story. Said Stewart to a *Chicago Daily News* reporter: "He was a shy old country boy. . . . He never said a word. They would say, 'Otis, go get us lunch,' or something like that." Then they gave him a chance to sing. "He did one of those 'Heh, heh, baby' things. . . . I told them the world didn't need another Little Richard. Then someone suggested he do a slow one. He did 'These Arms of Mine.' No one flipped over it."

No one may have flipped over it, but this tune, which Otis composed, marked the end of his road-managing days. In fact, it sold 800,000 copies and made the road manager a star. "Possibly the greatest and most-loved soul singer of the sixties." say critics Lenny Kaye and David Dalton. Right up there with James Brown, says Jon Landau in *Rolling Stone*. Right up there, say others, with Sam Cooke.

Where Cooke polished his act through his years of working the gospel circuit before entering the pop arena, Otis performed more or less from the gut. These different styles have obscured Cooke's influence on Otis, even in the ballads. Much more obvious is the influence of Otis's number-two hero, Little Richard. On Redding's first recordings, it is sometimes hard to tell them apart. Understanding this affinity helps explain the roughness. But Otis wanted more. He wanted to be polished. But basically, as Jon Landau says, Redding was a folk artist, working, not from a basis in technique, but from his own experience, from his own deeply felt emotional truth. He expressed himself with the instrument he had at hand. Even when he became a sophisticated technician as a vocalist, composer, and studio producer, his sophistication was built on a deep personal foundation.

Not coincidentally perhaps, both Otis and Richard (and Ray Charles) came from the area around Macon, Georgia. Otis was born in Dawson, some 20 miles from Macon, on September 9, 1941, into modest circumstances. Beyond that, little is known of his childhood. As a teenager, he listened to the radio, followed Little Richard, the hometown boy made good, and picked up odd jobs, always trying his best to get into show business, always with an idea that someday he might get to sing. One day he picked up an odd job driving for Johnny Jenkins and the Pinetoppers, who would sometimes let him sing. Then Johnny Jenkins went to the Stax studio in Memphis. End of odd jobs.

It only heightens the tragedy of his death that Otis Redding was so *alive*. On the black "chitlin" circuit where he spent the early years of his career, Otis's reputation as a live performer was rivaled only by that of James Brown. Otis's characteristic pose onstage was on his knees, coiled, sweat pouring down his face, in agony and ecstasy at the same time, a spirit bent to the breaking point but never broken. As a recording like "Satisfaction" partly captures, he was energy incarnate. He was heat.

While he was a star in black America, he was largely unknown by whites. When he covered the Beatles' "Day Tripper" and the Stones' "Satisfaction" he made it clear that he was unhappy with that situation and was determined to rectify it. But oddly enough, his big breakthrough in white America would come not for his covers of white artists' songs, not for his singing, but for his songwriting. Otis broke through with a song he had written and recorded back in 1965 and that in 1967 became the first and greatest hit of a young gospel-style singer named Aretha Franklin: "Respect." And while it didn't exactly make Otis's career in white rock, it helped bring his type of rough-hewn Memphis soul to the forefront of black music and from there to the top of white pop. At the same time, it gave Otis the confidence that he could make it in white rock.

It also gave his white manager and record company enough confidence to finally put some serious money behind him and work on a strategy. So later in 1967, working according to that strategy, Otis Redding became one of a handful of black performers to appear at the Monterey Pop Festival, where, along with a guitarist named Jimi Hendrix and a singer named Janis Joplin, Otis Redding tore the place up. Now he was poised to become white heat.

Otis had conquered soul. All he had to do was reach out and the brass ring was his. He could be *totally* commercial. But that's not the way Otis was.

Otis Redding was a folk artist. He had to be true to himself before all else. In late 1967, Otis Redding, who was gaining fame for his roughness and speed, went in and recorded the smoothest ballad he had ever done, with a beat that was literally the lapping sea. It had the equally gentle, introspective title of "Dock of the Bay," in tribute to the warmth he had found by the bay at the Monterey Pop Festival. Everybody thought he was crazy. Not that everyone didn't recognize its beauty; they just knew it wasn't commercial. Otis, however, persisted. But when he left on a tour across the Midwest that winter, the record company still wasn't sure, and "Dock of the Bay" remained in limbo.

On December 10, 1967—three years (less one day), eerily enough, since Sam Cooke had taken a chestful of slugs in L.A.— Otis Redding and five of the Bar-Kays, his backing horn group, hopped a twin-engine Beechcraft to make it across Lake Michigan to a gig in Madison, Wisconsin.

Madison was a college town where there were lots of young whites turning on to new music and lately to new *black* music like Otis Redding's. But you wouldn't see James Brown in Madison. You wouldn't even see Aretha. It was a bold move by a man who managed to reach out to broader audiences without sacrificing his integrity. Over the lake that afternoon, the fog suddenly started rolling in, and the pilot became confused. In an attempt to see better, he took the plane down lower. Air controllers saw a blip go off their radar screens. It never returned.

Only twenty-year-old Ben Cauley of the Bar-Kays survived the crash. He heard two of his fellow band members call for help as the craft went under the icy water, but he was unable to reach them. Otis Redding was among the five drowned—the heat extinguished by ice. Otis Redding, who always looked and sounded older than his years, was barely twenty-six.

There can be no doubt that it took a lot to douse the fire that was Otis Redding. He did not die without a bitter struggle. Surely this feeling is confirmed by the grisly police photos that show the body being hoisted from the lake. In one, Otis's elbow rests on the edge of the dredging barge almost as if on the edge of his corner bar. His shoulders are hunched from the pull of the harness, but that makes him look even larger than he always seemed to be. Above the shoulders, the head tilts forward slightly in a Christ-like attitude. But even with the eyes closed, the face betrays not resignation, but disappointment, bitterness even. The expression is not *Why me?*, as it is on so many cadavers; it's *Not me,* as though he put up one hell of a fight.

In January 1968, after consulting with numerous music-biz professionals—reportedly including none other than *Rolling Stone*'s number-one Otis fan, Jon Landau—the record company agreed to take a chance and issue Otis's last recording as a single. By May, the gentle, wistful song with the lapping-sea beat— ironic, considering his watery demise—had gone to number one on the white pop charts, sold 4 million copies, and made Otis Redding a complete star. Said his record company's president in 1968 of "Dock of the Bay": "It's his epitaph, and it proves that a singer can do his own thing and still be commercially successful. Otis is tremendously responsible for the fact that . . . the young white audience now digs soul the way the black does."

7

BRIAN JONES

No Satisfac- tion

*I*magine *you* were he. You're twenty-one, twenty-two, twenty-three years old. You've got a ton of money. And you've got the whole world at your feet, including girls. Everyone wants something from you, but at the same time, you want it, too, if only because you can just about have it all.

This was the time before celebrity got so cheap. Not everybody got on TV. And rock 'n' roll was poised to make a new world. It's a wonder all the big guys didn't die. Just *imagine* you were a Rolling Stone. Imagine, in fact, that you were *the* Rolling Stone. Imagine a dream—that turned into a nightmare and a curse.

"After we had split up," said Linda Lawrence, his first love, "I said I wanted to try it again. Brian said he didn't think so because he was going to die before he was thirty. . . . It was as if he had just seen a doctor and been told he had some terminal illness."

He did. He was Brian Jones, *the* Brian Jones. And on July 3, 1969, at the tender age of twenty-six, he died of it.

Brian Jones conceived of the Rolling Stones and then rode that rollicking concept to its logical conclusion. He lived out what Mick Jagger and Keith Richards (more or less) only stood for. He

was the excess and the first major casualty of the sixties. To see him on the sleeve of his last single with the band, "Jumpin' Jack Flash," laughing dementedly beneath that golden hair, Satan's pitchfork in one hand and a martini in the other, is to see the man who embodied The Scene. Yet he was a real musician, too. Despite all his latter-day posing, despite the drugs and drinking and illegitimate children and all of it, a musician was what Brian most wanted to be.

Lewis Brian Hopkins-Jones was born on February 28, 1942, in Cheltenham, England, a pretty, staid, middle-class English village about a hundred miles from London. His father, Lewis, was an aeronautical engineer; his mother, Louise, a part-time piano teacher and a housewife. Academically, Brian did not excel in school, despite an IQ of 135. Socially, Brian did somewhat better, at least with the girls. At seventeen, he got his high school girlfriend pregnant and, in what was to be a turning point (no doubt for *both* of them), dropped out of school. These, one must remember, were more decorous times. Indeed, these were times before rock 'n' roll stars like Brian Jones had savaged the social codes of Western civilization.

Brian discovered jazz at a coffeehouse hangout in Cheltenham. Shortly thereafter he began listening to his beloved blues. He also began to learn to play guitar with a vengeance he would later only reluctantly relinquish to drugs.

"Brian was the first person I heard playing the slide electric guitar," Keith Richards explained to an interviewer. "He played with Alexis [Korner, Britain's white blues godfather] one night at the Ealing Club. Mick and I both thought he was incredible. Mick went up to talk to him for a bit. That's when Brian mentioned he was forming a band."

The band Brian dreamed up, carefully put together and named after a favorite Muddy Waters song, was the Rolling Stones. And Brian was its leader. Or, as former Stones intimate and codemimondaine Tony Sanchez puts it: "In the early sixties Brian was king. Mick and Keith vied for his friendship as he tried to teach them both all he knew about music."

Brian had a feeling the Rolling Stones could also rule the

kingdom, and it was a feeling he managed to impart to his new friends and pupils. "We knew all along, you see," Brian told Sanchez. "People were getting sick of traditional jazz, and they were looking around for something different—and we all knew that something was us."

And it was: In 1963, the Stones were the hottest club band in London. Within a year they released their first Decca single, a very different version of Buddy Holly's "Not Fade Away," and became the hottest club band in the world. Unfortunately, as Keith Richards tells it, "Brian peaked when we were the hottest band in London."

In 1965, they released their second album, which contained their first number-one U.S. hit, a tune written by Jagger and Richards called "The Last Time." It was the beginning of the end of Brian's influence in the band, although he didn't yet realize it. According to Sanchez: "Brian was still loving it all then, in 1965. He was the beautiful Stone, the one the fans screamed over while they told jokes about 'old rubber lips' Jagger.

"He seemed to have become . . . almost content," Sanchez continues ominously. "Until the foxiest blonde I had ever seen arrived in London."

No story of the decline and fall of Brian Jones would be complete without the Italian-German beauty and sometime actress Anita Pallenberg. In many of the theories of why this young man of such promise died desperate, she ranks right up there with Mick, Keith, and Scotland Yard as a primary cause. She is, according to many, the villainess of the Brian Jones story.

But, to tell the truth, no one came better suited to such a role. Says Sanchez: "She had only to walk along the street to cause a string of traffic accidents. She had tumbling, shining blonde hair, a long, lithe body and wickedly beautiful cat's eyes. She was no dumb blonde either." One need only watch the movie *Performance*, in which she and Jagger play decadent people not unlike themselves, to be persuaded of her power.

One old friend elaborated on Brian and Anita and the London hip scene of 1965: "Brian threw himself in at the deep end. At that particular time he was out for as many kicks as he could get. Anita was great. She excited Brian—whatever young guys only read about he was getting on a plate. She was into the bisexual number and arranged scenes."

Sanchez continues, "As a couple, Brian and Anita exuded an almost surrealistic aura: They began to look, dress, and think so much alike that they became one—a single presence in silk and satin." But there was another side. "They each carried a cruel streak in their nature, the seed of self-destruction."

They laughed and shut Linda Lawrence out of the house when she came with Brian's baby seeking money and help. They dressed Brian up in a Nazi uniform and had him stomp a doll with his jackboot and sent a photo to the papers. An antifascist protest, they said—a joke. So why didn't everybody think it was funny? They pouted. They stood above it all and above everybody. Brian and Anita cackled together into the howling winds of decadence—which waited to swallow them up. Anita was trapped no less than Brian, but somehow, by so many accounts, she was the *true* devil in disguise.

Ironically, the worst thing that this allegedly wicked, wanton woman did to Brian was to leave him. This theory is the one that his father, Lewis, would later propound on a British radio show. "What I firmly believe," said Lewis of his son, "was that when he lost the only girl he ever loved, this was a very severe blow to him. He changed suddenly and alarmingly—from a bright, enthusiastic young man to a quiet and morose and inward-looking young man. And it was at that time I believe that he got mixed up with drugs, if indeed he was. Whether he just took to drugs in the way many people take to drink . . . I don't know. . . . I am convinced and always shall be convinced that was the turning point in Brian's life, rather than the pop scene generally."

Father Lewis is being naive about the drugs, of course. Brian was well along in his personal drug research by the start of his relationship with Anita. In 1965, during the Stones' second American tour and then again during their third, in 1966, Brian had already missed several dates when he was hospitalized for drug overdoses, presumably downs. But it was probably with

Anita, perhaps only by happenstance, that Brian first took acid, a point that, according to Sanchez, also "marked the peak of Brian's brief life and the start of his personality disintegration. . . . On LSD, he told me, he was able to write songs and play guitar the way he had always dreamed."

Acid meant a lot to Brian, and Brian eventually made sure acid meant a lot to the Stones. Brian introduced Keith to acid, and acid brought the two of them closer together than they had ever been. Acid also helped him lose his girlfriend to his best mate, and the band to Mick. The Stones' relationships to one another deteriorated, prompting Tony Sanchez to comment to Mick and Keith, "Seems like you and Mick hardly ever speak to Brian anymore." And Keith reportedly replied: "Well, he's burned out, isn't he?"

"After about the third year," Keith told Jones biographer Mandy Aftel, "Brian was very disinterested in the music because having to play Jagger–Richards compositions bruised his ego." In lieu of music, and besides drugs (which had become merely a normal state for Brian by 1966), Brian cultivated an interest in travel, particularly to dreamy, druggy Tangier, Morocco. Tangier was his retreat, his escape, a place to regain his equilibrium.

But of course, being utterly without discipline anymore and mostly without sense, he usually brought along everything that he was attempting to escape from and spent most of his days high on his own stash, augmented by the cheap local hash. After the first Rolling Stones bust, in February 1967, when the police missed arresting Brian at a party at Keith's only because Brian turned out to be too stoned to attend, he even brought Keith to Tangier, or vice versa.

After the bust, Keith said, "Everybody felt, 'Oh, what a bring-down. Let's all go to Morocco, take a load off, and cheer up.' . . . Me, Brian, Anita, and [friend] Deborah Dixon decided to drive down in my Bentley. At this time Brian and Anita weren't getting along.

"We were driving through France on the way to Morocco and Brian fell sick. Whereas everybody else was buzzing on this incredible high, Brian was going his other way. I think it was genuinely directed at calling for Anita's attention or something. It was just such a weird trip over the Pyrenees into Spain. Brian got this terror of mountains. It was an asthmatic thing, which is all psychosomatic and mixed up with the head thing. After he collapsed we stayed a couple of days with him to see how he was getting on. Then the doctors said, 'Oh, yes . . . he's in a bad way. He'll be here a week.' We said, 'Oh . . . um . . . this, that, and the other . . . we'd better go.' "

While Keith's leaving might sound cruel or negligent, it's worth remembering that taking care of Brian Jones had become a full-time job. Keith and the others may have simply decided that their own lives must go on. In any case, after the week was up, Anita retrieved Brian and finally got him to Morocco. But for what?

Evidently, Brian and Anita were fighting again, with Brian now making passes at Moroccan women, and Keith could not stand watching it. "We arranged for somebody to take him off and listen to some Moroccan musicians—long enough for us to spring out of town with him hot on our tracks." Of course, Keith omits the fact that he was by then completely in love with Anita and that abandoning Brian and taking his girl was something more than cold-blooded. It was treachery of the highest order.

Brian was crushed to discover that his best friends had left him. "He searched the room frantically for a note, some word or explanation. . . . He ran down to the main desk asking, 'Is there any note for me? Did my friends leave any forwarding address?' Nothing. He dashed back up to the room sobbing and yelling at the same time." But if Keith was (to put it mildly) inconsiderate of Brian, who did Brian ever consider?

You are twenty-four, twenty-five years old. You've got a ton of money and the whole world at your feet, including girls. But it's wearing a little thin. You'll take any drug that is offered and then some, and you spend most of your time stoned. One only has to look at the photos, the smirking, puffy-eyed photos, to know. You are stoned, and you are arrogant, too. Pretty soon, your girlfriend is not going to be your biggest problem.

Scotland Yard came down on Brian on May 10, 1967, like a ton of bricks. They busted him and a friend for possession of cannabis, Methedrine, and cocaine. It was a nice little offense, and they were going to nail him for the smirking photos and for the Rolling Stones. Mick and Keith were still out on bail from their bust. Jagger saw a conspiracy. Drugs and the Stones, he told Sanchez, had been made "synonymous" in the public mind.

Now out on bail himself, Brian removed himself from the scene. He went to America to introduce his new friend Jimi Hendrix at the Monterey Pop Festival. As the movie *Monterey Pop* shows, there's no doubt about whether Brian mended his ways: He is puffy-eyed and smirking *extraordinaire*. Shortly after Monterey, back home in England, Brian suffered a nervous breakdown. His post-Anita girlfriend, model Suki Potier, described his general state before the breakdown proper: "He had this incredible conviction he wouldn't live very long. . . . George Harrison told him, 'Action brings reaction—what you've done in one life, you'll pay for in the next.' And Brian would say, 'God, what could I have done in my last life to have it get me like this?''

Released from the nursing home where he was supposed to have recovered from his breakdown, Brian remained as paranoid as ever: "I understand now what Mick and Keith are doing," he said. "They want to prove that they are better than I am."

Dr. Green, the psychiatrist who treated him, told him more or less the same thing (less the paranoia). "This is why I was trying to encourage him to get out and record his Arab [Moroccan] music—because he had to have something for himself. . . . He didn't even have girlfriends that were all his own. . . . "

Dr. Green's diagnosis: "I don't think Brian was living in a real world."

On October 30, Brian's case finally went to trial. A plea bargain had been worked out. The prosecution would drop the cocaine and Methedrine charges in exchange for Brian's guilty plea to possession of marijuana and allowing his premises to be used for smoking it, both relatively minor offenses. Brian pleaded guilty, and what happened next shocked everybody. The judge promptly sentenced him to nine months in jail, and off he went in the paddy wagon.

Brian Jones was released on bail pending appeal after one

night in Wormwood Scrubs. Over the next 10 weeks he was examined by three different psychiatrists, including Dr. Green, all of whom concluded he was seriously neurotic, with possible suicidal tendencies. One of them prepared an extensive written report that said in part: "He vacillates between a passive, dependent child with a confused image of an adult on the one hand, and an idol of pop culture on the other. He is very involved with Oedipal fixations . . . grasp on reality is fragile . . . it is very likely that his imprisonment could precipitate a complete break with reality, and significantly increase the suicidal risk for this man."

In the face of this, duly reported in London's famous tabloids, the judge relented, letting Brian off with a fine and three years' probation. Had this suicidal neurotic pop idol learned his lesson? Writes Sanchez, "He celebrated his release by pouring bottles full of pills into his mouth . . . acid, coke, speed. . . . Then, after a day and night of being totally strung out, he went to a club in Covent Garden with one of his many women. . . . The resident band invited him to play with them. . . . He picked up a big double bass and started to play it fluidly, though as he played, he kicked it with his Cuban-heeled boots until it was smashed to matchwood.

"Brian was so far gone that he carried on playing an invisible instrument, pumping out beautiful music only he could hear. . . . Then he started to weep uncontrollably, and his girl was forced to shove him into a cab and take him home." And so on. The girlfriend finally called an ambulance, and when he seemed to come to his senses at the hospital, a doctor sent him home. What could the doctor do? No doubt about it, Brian Jones was simply terminal.

Like many a shining light before him, Brian flared again brightly and briefly before being extinguished for good. Brian's flaring, not coincidentally, was on the recording of the Stones' sixties masterpiece, *Beggars' Banquet*.

Banquet was the return to rock 'n' roll and blues that Brian had longed for, and apparently he threw himself into its making as much as he was capable of throwing himself into anything anymore. Mostly, says Aftel, he would call in sick and do goofballs. Unfortunately, *Banquet* came too late for Brian. He no longer led the group he had started, and by 1968 he was hardly even one of its members.

Brian returned to North Africa, where he recorded the Jajouka tribesmen for an album eventually released as a tribute by Rolling Stones Records. He was otherwise, in an associate's terms, "non compos mentis." He traveled to Ceylon (now Sri Lanka), where he threw a temper tantrum when the two major hotels turned him away for being a crazy-looking "beatnik." He even visited Keith at his English country castle, where, shouting "I'm going to kill myself!" he dove into the moat—to be rescued by an angry Mick Jagger. Brian was particularly despondent because of something else that happened in 1968: He was busted again.

Mick later told *Crawdaddy* magazine: "Now if you do that kind of thing to some people it makes them strong and if you do it to others it can quickly destroy them, and it destroyed Brian which is very sad. . . . Brian came really close to doing six months. . . . He was followed all the time, but we all were. It was a systematic campaign of harassment [and it] brought Brian down. . . . "

After *Banquet*, Brian participated in the Stones' never-aired all-star TV film *The Rock 'n' Roll Circus,* which featured the Stones, John and Yoko, the Who, Eric Clapton, and Marianne Faithful, among others. Carrying a flute and wearing a magician's robe, Brian was to say one line: "Here come the clowns." By several accounts, he almost didn't get it out. Brian's behavior was described as "pathetic." It turned out to be his swan song with the Rolling Stones.

In January 1969, Brian was acquitted of the latest drug charge and he retired to his new suburban estate, Cotchford Farm, once owned by A. A. Milne, creator of Winnie-the-Pooh. There, says one latter-day girlfriend, Brian was getting much better, cutting down on the drugs, when Mick and Keith arrived to force the issue of his membership in the band. They told him they wanted to go on tour. He told them he couldn't handle it. All of them agreed to say that Brian had split with the Stones, while providing the option to return and a $300,000-a-year stipend. Guilt money, say the Mick and Keith haters. In any case, nobody, including a bitter Brian, expected the fair-haired boy to come back. Instead, he planned to form a bigger, better, blusier band.

On the night of July 2, 1969, Brian Jones took a dive for the last time. Three other people—his new Swedish girlfriend, Anna; Frank Thorogood, a builder charged with the renovation of Brian's estate; and Janet Lawson, a nurse friend of Thorogood— were definitely there. It was a party—but then it was always a party with Brian. A lot of liquor was consumed, especially by Brian and Thorogood, and the now ex–Rolling Stone supplemented the booze with his usual assortment of downs. Around midnight he decided they should adjourn to the swimming pool, over Janet Lawson's protestations. Anna and Thorogood went into the pool with Brian, while Lawson stayed in the house. What happened next is hazy. Anna got out of the pool to answer the phone, one story goes, or perhaps to get a cigarette, and a few minutes later Thorogood got out to find a towel. At which point Janet Lawson returned to the pool and screamed.

Brian Jones lay motionless underwater. Anna and Thorogood retrieved him, and Nurse Lawson applied external heart massage. Anna performed mouth-to-mouth resuscitation. "While we were doing this," Anna said, "I actually felt his hand grip mine." Eventually an ambulance was called, but all to no avail. Brian Jones had lived the Stones myth to its inevitable conclusion.

He did not die of an asthma attack, as was initially reported. The clinical circumstances surrounding his death, reported by pathologist Dr. Albert Sachs at a press conference a week later, were as follows: "His heart was fat and flabby. His liver was twice the normal weight . . . and not functioning properly. . . . I could find no evidence microscopically that he had had an attack of asthma." According to coroner Angus Sommerville, Brian's death was the result of "immersion in fresh water under the influence of drugs and alcohol." Or, as the investigators would stamp it, "death by misadventure."

Two days later, the Rolling Stones—now including Mick Taylor—played a previously scheduled free concert in London's Hyde Park. Billed now as a tribute to Brian, the concert attracted hundreds of thousands, many in tears, and Jagger opened it by releasing a boxful of white butterflies and reading from Shelley's romantic poem about early death, "Adonais":

Peace, peace! he is not dead, he doth not sleep—
He hath awakened from the death of life. . . .

Brian's life was indeed a dream—a dark one spun in a chemical twilight devoid finally of love and dignity, the dream of a rare, fatal fever known as Brian Jonesitis.

8

JIMI HENDRIX

Up from the Skies

Of them all, Jimi Hendrix, a dues-paid pro and show-biz vet, should have known better. Then again, maybe he did. "It's funny the way most people love the dead," he was heard to observe in 1968. "Once you are dead, you are made for life." So maybe Hendrix, the crafty old show-bizzer, *did* off himself. Not for the cosmic reasons that Eric Burdon ascribed, but simply as a crafty old show-biz stunt, as a way to even greater acclaim, as the step beyond burning your guitar: burning yourself. It's possible—but doubtful. Jimi didn't need such stunts. He was "made for life" as a musician and guitar player whether he was dead or alive.

Jimi probably just fucked up. He took too many drugs for too many years, and then he took too many drugs one night and wound up aspirating vomit into his windpipe. Also known as choking on your own puke.

Jimi Hendrix was born on November 27, 1942, in Seattle. Al Hendrix, his father, had tried to make a career as a professional dancer, and once had even danced with Louis Armstrong's band, before giving it all up. It was on a Seattle dance floor that Jimi's father met his mother, Lucille, who seemed to harbor similar show-biz aspirations, but lacked the confidence to pursue them.

Jimi's love of music was rooted in family tradition.

His love of getting fucked up was also rooted in family tradition—specifically as set down by Lucille. Just seven months after the birth of her first son she was back in the hospital, recovering from a drunken tear that came close to killing her. Her drinking and running off with other men went a long way toward ruining her marriage to Al and leaving Jimi a victim of a bitterly broken home.

While Jimi wasn't sent to foster homes, as was his younger brother, Leon, he did spend a lot of time fending for himself. And teaching himself trouble. Luckily though, he also taught himself something else: the guitar.

No one, however, would have bet money as to which was his *true* vocation. His first big trouble came when he was thrown out of high school for sassing a teacher. "I was talking to some chick during the lessons and this teacher got mad," he explained. "I said, 'What's the matter, are you jealous?'" He was also arrested twice in one week for stealing cars.

And he got high. "We liked that cough syrup," an old friend says. "It had codeine in it, and that's the best high except for the really heavy stuff. Half the people on that corner turned into dope fiends. I was a junkie sixteen years. Half of them guys . . . are dead today. Back then, we drank the cough syrup, passing the bottle around, then went back to school and nodded out in study hall."

In 1961, he enlisted in the army. Jimi met a bass player named Billy Cox there, and when the two were discharged they went together to make it in Nashville. From there, separately and together, they traveled to hundreds of other cities, with dozens of different musicians, behind a wide variety of bandleaders and front men, and for three years Jimi Hendrix learned musical discipline.

After a long stint with Little Richard, he dropped out and landed in New York in 1964. He kept body and soul together working the metropolitan area as guitarist with Curtis Knight and the Squires. To pick up the slack, he dealt drugs.

He occupied his days and nights drinking in the music and the atmosphere of the fabulous city that never sleeps. Some of the music he drank in was Bob Dylan's, and in 1965, in emulation of Dylan, Hendrix started hanging out in Greenwich Village, eventually putting together his own band, Jimmy James and the Blue Flames, and copping a regular gig at the Cafe Wha?. He also met a steamy tropical inversion by the name of Devon Wilson.

Devon did many things for Jimi, according to those who knew her. Curtis Knight said Devon was "magnetic . . . attractive, and totally into sex—proficient, imaginative—from A to Z." Devon herself admitted that she also turned Jimi on with other things, including LSD. "He liked it a lot," she said. "He tried various pills with me, and our relationship became one of excitement and exhilaration."

But according to a somewhat more graphic friend of Devon's, she mostly turned him on with sex. "She really dug him, you know. And it wasn't just the size of his meat that attracted her, like it pulled a lot of other chicks. Jimi was big . . . and that was important—Devon liked her men well hung—but she said he was also the best. . . . Devon told me they were staying in one of those terrible midtown hotels, and Jimi got it up and kept it up all night long. They were doing a lot of blow, and it was like his cock was frozen solid. She said she taught him a lot that night, showed him 'around the world' and a lotta other tricks. You know, like deep throat. Devon was into that years before Linda What's-Her-Name. . . . " And thus began Jimi's legendary sexual career.

Meanwhile, back in the Village, Jimi's other career was also set to take off. John Hammond, Jr., Mike Bloomfield, the Animals, and the Rolling Stones had heard about this hot young blues and R & B guitarist at the Cafe Wha?. He was an honest-to-God black man, a *real* blues man, and they trooped down to check him out. "I was the hot-shot guitarist on the block," Bloomfield told *Guitar Player* magazine. "I'd never heard of Hendrix. . . . He just got right up in my face with that axe and I didn't even want to pick up a guitar for the next year." Chas Chandler, bassist for the Animals, had another epiphany upon seeing Hendrix. He wanted to manage him.

Chandler quit the Animals that summer of 1966 and got Jimmy, who at Chas's suggestion became "Jimi," to go to England with him. Chandler helped him put together and name the Experience and cut a single, and he used all his influence and just about all his money to spread Hendrix's reputation around hip London. Hendrix's talent made it a lot easier.

By the beginning of 1967, when that first single, "Hey Joe," entered the U.K. charts, Hendrix had become "*the* new guitar in town. . . . All the birds were falling all over him. Even Mick Jagger felt threatened. A lot of that had to do with Marianne Faithful. . . . " Or as the source says of London's hip society at the time: "Mick was the king and Marianne was the queen and Jimi was the jack of spades. It made for some of the best gossip available."

With a successful single, an album in England, and the furor caused by performances in which he set his guitar aflame, Jimi was ripe to return to America. He had not been treated kindly by the British press. The sensation-mongering tabloids, with barely disguised racism, called him "the Wild Man of Pop" and "Mau-Mau."

In May 1967, he was signed to Reprise Records. A month later, at Paul McCartney's suggestion and introduced by his new friend Brian Jones, Jimi Hendrix returned to play California's Monterey Pop Festival. The straight executives of his American record company—until recently owned by Frank Sinatra—were blown away with embarrassment by Hendrix's overt sexuality and violent pyrotechnics (immortalized in the documentary *Monterey Pop*). But the crowd, including his fellow musicians, were blown away, period. Said the *L.A. Times* critic: "When Jimi left the stage, he had graduated from rumor to legend."

Jimi had indeed graduated. In Los Angeles after the Monterey show, he jammed with Steve Stills, David Crosby, Neil Young, and Buddy Miles for three days in Stills's Malibu house. And then, perhaps not surprisingly, Crosby, Hendrix, and Stills, joined by Mike Bloomfield and with Stills at the wheel, wrecked Monkee Peter Tork's GTO. No one was seriously hurt.

Jimi graduated in other ways, too. "At first he never drank much," says manager Chandler. "Three whiskeys and he was happy." Now, Chas Chandler watched the alcohol intake accelerate. After Hendrix returned to England in the fall of 1967 to record the second LP, *Axis: Bold As Love*, Chas watched other intakes accelerate, too. "Eric Burdon was on his big acid scene then, but Jimi would just say, 'Oh, he's an acid freak' and put that whole scene down. It wasn't until the time of the second album that I realized he had in fact been taking it. He'd split for a couple of days, and I realized he was on acid. . . . Halfway through *Axis* . . . he was dropping it every day. I told him he'd have to be straight some of the time. At first I thought it would give him a new slant to his lyrics.

"We had an argument about it and he said, 'Okay, no more.' Then someone would turn up at the studio with a bag of goodies and pour some more down his throat."

While they were recording *Axis*, the Jimi Hendrix Experience undertook a massive 35-date European tour. Even for a seasoned hand like Jimi, the tour, on top of the recording on top of everything else, was a lot to handle. It all caught up with him on January 4, in a fancy hotel room in Gothenburg, Sweden. Biographer David Henderson describes the scene: "He had started drinking with the intent of getting drunk. Before he knew it he was a moving blackout. First he started on the glasses and the lamps, smashing them to smithereens. Then the chairs began to go out of the windows. Noel Redding had the room next to him and was the first to realize what was happening. Jim was stoned and drunk and not easy to handle. He had a wild wiriness with incredibly strong arms. [Road manager] Gerry Stickells came in, and soon he and Noel had wrestled Jimi to the floor and sat on him.

"The hotel authorities were outraged. . . . Although Chas Chandler offered to make full payment for the wrecked room, the hotel authorities insisted on arresting Jimi. . . . The police insisted on handcuffing him, arguing that he was violent. They made one concession: They allowed Jimi to wear his handcuffs in front of him instead of behind his back. Jimi was . . . escorted from the

Opelan Hotel . . . by two policemen. He walked between them with a white midlength fur coat thrown over his shoulders.'' The following morning, after a night in jail, continues Henderson, Hendrix "insisted to Chas that he remembered nothing of the incident—it had been a complete blackout.''

Axis: Bold As Love was released in February 1968 and climbed immediately into the Top 20, and Hendrix embarked on his first full-scale headlining tour of the U.S. One of the first dates was a triumphant homecoming concert in the Seattle Center Arena, attended by his father and brother. It was followed by the presentation of an honorary degree at Garfield High School—the same place from which Jimi, not too very long before, had been expelled.

While the entire student body looked on, the principal poured forth a principal-like speech, and then a popular local DJ introduced the honoree himself. Clearly uncomfortable, and probably stoned, Hendrix managed to get out that he was glad to be home. Staring at the assembly, he then concluded his valedictory by asking, "Are there . . . uh . . . any questions?'' Eventually, after much more silent discomfort, a brave young girl piped up, "How long have you been away from Seattle?'' To which Hendrix, after a reasonable ponder, replied: "Oh, for about five thousand years.'' And then he walked off. For not unimaginable reasons, he never did get that diploma. More than anything, the principal probably regretted he couldn't expel him all over again.

In Chicago, Jimi was given a different kind of reception. Returning to his hotel between shows (those being the days when even top-of-the-line rock stars played two shows per night), he was set upon by two friendly, albeit purposeful, young women who wanted him to take off his pants. But they weren't groupies, or not exactly. As was spelled out in tape on the side of their black attaché case, they were the Plaster Casters. To be visited by them was a sign that a musician in the sixties had truly arrived.

The Plaster Casters, quite simply, made plaster casts of rock 'n' roll stars' cocks. Which they promptly did this night in Chicago, as recorded quite clinically in their diary, after orally administering to an eager Jimi Hendrix. "We needed a ratio of

28:28 and found this just barely sufficient. He has got just about the biggest rig [British slang for cock] I've ever seen! We had to plunge him through the entire depth of the vase . . . we got a BEAUTIFUL mold. He even kept his hard for the entire minute. He got stuck, however, for about fifteen minutes (his hair did), but he was an excellent sport—didn't panic . . . he actually enjoyed it and balled the impression after it had set. In fact, I believe the reason we couldn't get his rig out was that it wouldn't GET SOFT! We rubbed a little warm water around the top of his balls, and eventually it slipped out. A beautiful (to say the least) mold with part of a ball and some random embedded hairs. . . . '' The legend marched on.

In October 1968, led by the single "All Along the Watchtower," Hendrix's classic cover of the Dylan tune, the new Jimi Hendrix Experience album hit the record stores and the airwaves. Called *Electric Ladyland*, it was Jimi's pièce de résistance. Coproduced, written, and mostly performed by the guitarist himself, *Ladyland* took his music over the top. At the same time, out on the road, his manager noted ominously that Jimi was "becoming unmanageable." Friends felt that Jimi had changed. He always wanted to be on center stage. The show-biz vet had made a (literally) fatal mistake: He'd begun to take it all a little too seriously.

Noel Redding said, "Screw 'im! I'm going home to me 'umble estate in County Cork.'' Telling friends he could no longer work with Jimi the way he had now become, Mitch Mitchell expressed similar disgust and went home to England, too. In the year of their greatest triumph—*Ladyland* had shipped a half million copies, and the reviews had been lavishly laudatory, with *Rolling Stone* naming him Performer of the Year—the Jimi Hendrix Experience, for all intents and purposes, ceased to exist. Thus, the end of 1968, the year of his greatest triumph, found Jimi Hendrix accelerating on a not-so-slow spiral to oblivion.

Spring 1969 brought more bad news. On his way to a gig in Toronto, Jimi was busted by Canadian police for heroin. A setup, everyone said. But it was a lot more serious than the usual pot or coke frame job. Hendrix could do time for smack. The heroin user was also not yet the romantic figure he was to become in the later seventies, and a heroin bust could do serious damage to the Hendrix image—that is to say, to his career and bankbook. Mysteriously, his protectors were able to manage the news of the bust and, of course, get him out on bail. Trial was set for the following December.

On July 3, Jimi's friend and sponsor Brian Jones washed up dead in his own swimming pool. "Jimi was visibly depressed," says biographer Hopkins, adding: "Typically, Jimi said nothing to friends. The only acknowledgment of Brian's death occurred during an appearance on Johnny Carson's 'Tonight' show. . . . Jimi introduced a new song called 'Lover Man' and dedicated it to his dead friend." Jimi's life was going down the tubes, and he knew it.

He went straight back to the music, to his guitar. For a while that summer, he could be found jamming with everybody in New York, from the Last Poets to Timothy Leary, the acid guru. Many of these sessions are preserved on the tapes of producer Alan Douglas, some of which have been posthumously released. Later Jimi moved the jams to his big stone house in Woodstock, New York, a few hours away. He was excited about the upcoming Woodstock festival. It jibed with some ideas he had.

Jimi was tired of the traditional band concept. He wanted to have a sort of free-floating, elastic musico-artistic commune, which he called his "electric sky church." But it wasn't to be. The attraction of communal life didn't have a prayer beside stardom and its perks. Besides, when word got around that it was Jimi Hendrix staying in the big stone house in the woods, the perks of stardom again came knock-knocking.

Ever since the Plaster Casters incident, publicized in a *Rolling Stone* feature on groupies, one of the main perks of Jimi's stardom had been sex. When word of the size of Jimi's "rig" got out, apparently all the groupies wanted to sample. Jimi's friend and Woodstock neighbor Jerry Morrison remembered one late-night phone call from Hendrix. "Hurry! I need help fast!" the cryptic, slightly panicked call concluded. Morrison hopped in his jeep and raced over, bounding upstairs and straight into the master bedroom. Panting, he took in the scene.

"Jimi had a huge bed, and there he was in the middle of it, covered by six or seven girls who were sucking on every orifice and protuberance."

Hendrix smiled at his out-of-breath buddy. "You a friend?" he asked.

"Yes," replied Jerry Morrison.

"Well, do me a favor . . . "

Said Jerry, "Anything . . . "

Said Jimi Hendrix, "Well, take off your clothes and join me."

After the Woodstock festival, while Jimi was away in New York, some other fans found the stone house and broke in, leaving their idol a message in spray paint on the bedroom wall. Jerry Morrison reported the vandalism to Hendrix, who began berating him in a characteristic reaction.

"Lemme think. . . . It said, 'Jimi, you shoulda been here. I give the greatest head.' And then it was signed—dammit, Jimi, I can't remember. . . . "

"Damn," said Hendrix. "The girl says she's the best cock-sucker in the world and you forget her name. . . . " No one ever accused Jimi Hendrix of being particularly kind toward women.

In Canada the following December, after much trepidation on Jimi's part, a UPI reporter took the stand and confirmed Hendrix's alibi. Jimi said he had been given the drugs by a fan and hadn't paid any attention when he threw them in a suitcase. Yes, he had once taken drugs, Jimi himself testified, but now he had "outgrown" them. The Toronto jury found Jimi Hendrix not guilty. Needless to say, it was a tremendous relief. And for a brief moment, say friends, Jimi was happy again and threw himself into assembling a new group, Band of Gypsies, with Buddy Miles and Billy Cox. For a brief moment.

His management team had fallen apart. Chas Chandler had been ousted in favor of partner Mike Jeffery. Jeffery didn't think Band of Gypsies was the right commercial vehicle. Other typical show-biz legal hassles accrued. Hendrix wobbled a bit under the pressure and headed for the high hills of his own head. Said

Buddy Miles: "In those days he was out there. . . . Grass, hash, acid, coke, booze, everything. He was a glutton. One time . . . we had a fight. I picked him up by his collar. I said, 'Jimi, what are you doing? Is this all that life is—drugs?' He told me I was right, but he said he was afraid."

The most harrowing event of Jimi's tragic slide down occurred at the Band of Gypsies' second gig, a Madison Square Garden benefit for the antiwar movement. Someone, it seems, gave Hendrix some very bad acid. A "couple" of tabs, says Buddy Miles, that "cramped up his stomach" and "brought him to his knees." Johnny Winter, who was also performing, tells what he witnessed backstage:

"When I saw him, it gave me chills. It was the most horrible thing I'd ever seen. He came in with his entourage of people, and it was like he was already dead. He just walked in—and even though Jimi and I weren't the greatest of friends, we always talked, always—and he came in with his head down, sat on the couch alone, and put his head in his hands. He didn't say a word to anybody, and no one spoke to him. He didn't move until it was time for the show. He really wanted to do that gig, but he never should have. It wasn't that it was bad, but his whole thing was inspiration, and there wasn't any. . . .

"Finally, right in the middle of a song, he just took his guitar off, sat on the stage—the band was still playing—and told the audience, 'I'm sorry, we just can't get it together.' One of his people said he was sick and led him off the stage. He was just so unhappy that there was no way that he could play the show. It didn't have anything to do with the group. He had already died."

It was the last Band of Gypsies concert. Thereafter, Hendrix capitulated and allowed his manager to fire the band and reconvene the Experience. The press, and no doubt the fans, were skeptical. The move seemed too commercially calculated—those were still the days when a band was supposed to be somewhat of a spiritual grouping. The release of the movie *Woodstock* at this time briefly boosted Jimi's stock, but the Experience tour, while a commercial success, was not critically well received. Because Jimi knew the critics were right, that hurt. At the same time, Jimi and his management were making their own films, one a straight concert movie called *Jimi at Berkeley,* the other an elaborate psychedelic pseudophilosophic fantasy mishmash shot in Hawaii and called *Rainbow Bridge.* In a monologue that seemed to reflect his, to put it mildly, detached state of mind in Hawaii, Hendrix at one point in *Bridge* explains his out-of-body experiences. Says Jimi:

"It seems like there's this little center in space that's just rotating, you know, constantly rotating, and there's these souls on it, and you're sitting there like cattle at a water hole, and there's no rap actually going on, there's no emotions that are strung out, so you're just sitting there, and all of a sudden the next thing you know you'll be drawn to a certain thing, and the light gets bright and you see stuff, a page being turned, and you see yourself next to a Viet Cong, you know, a soldier being shot down, and all of a sudden you feel like helping that soldier up, but you're feeling yourself held in another vibe, another sense of that soldier.

"It seems like the soul of him, you know, and then you whisk back to the water hole or the oasis, and you're sitting there and you're rapping again or something, eating a banana cream pie and sitting on the gray hardwood benches and so forth, and all of a sudden somebody calls out again, but this is without words, that whole scene, and all of a sudden the next thing you know you see yourself looking down at the left paw of the Sphinx and the tomb of King Blourr and his friendly falcons and these all-night social workers with mattresses tied around their backs screaming, 'Curb service! Curb service!' You know, with a third eye in the middle of the pyramid.'' Budgeted at around $250,000, the movie would wind up costing $1 million—and still make no sense.

Enthralled with the studio, Electric Lady, he had built under Greenwich Village's funky Eighth Street, Hendrix spent long hours working on a new double album that he was calling *First Rays of the New Rising Sun.* He was almost finished when he ventured out for a series of concerts in the U.S. and Europe. The first was a would-be urban Woodstock on Randall's Island in the

East River beside Manhattan. Due to a variety of Woodstock-like snafus, headliner Hendrix did not appear until five in the morning.

The promoter described how the star occupied his time. "He was consuming drugs nonstop. He was drinking. He was smoking grass and snorting coke. He may have had some heroin, because I know there was some in the room: Several of those with him were heavily into it. I remember Mike Jeffery coming up to me over and over again. He kept saying, 'Put him on! Put him on or he won't make it!'"

Weeks later, Jimi arrived in Denmark for one of the last concerts on the tour. He was quite thoroughly the worse for wear. Stopping midway through his second number, he looked down at his audience and said, "I've been dead a long time." And he walked off. A biker riot at the next date, in Germany, caused that concert to be cut short and bassist Billy Cox to freak out completely, allegedly from LSD. In anguish over the vegetable-like condition of his old army buddy and otherwise generally burned out, Hendrix despaired. "Oh, God!" he cried out. He had reached the final fork in his road.

Jimi now took the fork that went to London, where he thought he could get help for Cox and hang out and relax. He talked to the press, saying that he was through with the outrageous clothes and jewelry and that he wanted to get back to being a musician. "I don't want to be a clown!" was how he had earlier put it. Trying to put his life in order, he found he couldn't stop thinking about Billy, or about the hostile, artistically stifling situation with his managers. As it turned out, London wasn't so great after all. He tried to make it better by seeing a lot of old friends, but, as one of them said, "He didn't seem like his old self."

Jimi then started to party. On September 16, he spent most of the night with blond skating star Monika Danneman at his side. After a nap at another friend's flat, he returned to Monika on the 17th and decided to explain to her his theory about the highest form of consciousness. The theory encompassed Martin Luther King and Geronimo and Hitler and the numbers nine and four and was more or less incoherent. "Remember this," he said to Monika solemnly, as if he were trying to say something else, something more, "this is the grand design."

After some shopping, Monika and Jimi hooked up briefly with old friends who laid some goofballs and a snort of powdered acid on him. They actually got back to Monika's early, around eight-thirty, and she cooked them both a nice quiet, romantic meal with a little wine. Rather than go to bed, however, Jimi then had Monika drop him off, around two in the morning, at someone's apartment. Per his instructions, Monika returned at three, like some kind of midnight mommy, to take him home.

"When we came back," says Monika, "we were talking. I took a sleeping tablet at about 7:00 A.M. I made him two fish sandwiches. We were in bed, talking. I woke about 10:20 A.M. He was sleeping normally. I went around the corner to get cigarettes. When I came back, he had been sick. He was breathing and his pulse was normal, but I could not wake him. I saw that he had taken sleeping tablets. There were nine of mine missing."

Worried that Hendrix would wake up and get angry if she made a big scene and took him to a hospital, she phoned Eric Burdon for advice. Eric advised the hospital, immediately. Eric's girlfriend, another old Hendrix pal, met Monika and the ambulance at the hospital, and after several tense minutes, a doctor emerged to tell them that the twenty-seven-year-old black male they had registered under a phony name was dead.

The coroner ruled that death was "a result of inhalation of vomit due to barbiturate intoxication." Eric Burdon went on TV—high on acid, he now admits—to say that Jimi "made his exit when he wanted to. His death was deliberate. He was happy dying. He used a drug to phase himself out of life and go someplace else." But the fact is that the most brilliant guitarist of his generation, the era's one true, certifiable genius of sound, took pills when he was already too high to know what he was taking and drowned—stupidly, unesthetically—in his own foul puke.

JIM MORRISON

The End as Prologue

I don't know how many times I'd be watching TV and he'd come sit on my face and fart. Or after drinking chocolate milk or orange juice, which makes your saliva real gooey, he'd put his knees on my shoulders so I couldn't move and hang a goober over my face.

—Jim Morrison's younger brother, Andy

*J*im Morrison was an American. Like millions of his generation, his fellow Baby Boomers and postwar Americans, the young Jim Morrison had it all, just as he was supposed to. He had a nice house to live in—actually a succession of nice houses as his navy-officer father was continually reassigned—and lots of toys to fill it.

Jim Morrison was an American, and he would never be otherwise. Not in a thousand years. Not in an eternity—which is exactly where Jim Morrison now waits for want of exactly such knowledge. Jim Morrison wanted to be something else. He wanted to be a French poet. Or any kind of poet. He didn't want

to be an American rock 'n' roll star. This conflict eventually contributed greatly to his death.

Born in Melbourne, Florida, on December 8, 1943, he lived in Clearwater with his mother and grandparents while Dad was away helping fight the war in the Pacific. After the war, when Dad was taken into the Pentagon, the Morrisons moved to a comfy upper-middle-class suburb of Washington. There followed assignments in scenic Albuquerque, in San Francisco, in San Diego.

Jim did fairly well in his all-American high school and eventually went to junior college, back in Clearwater, from which he transferred, against his parents wishes, to UCLA film school.

Jim grew his hair long as the sixties progressed, and when his mother asked him to come meet his father at the harbor where the old man was returning from a long cruise, she also told him to get a haircut. "Your father's a captain now, Jim," his mother said. "There are three thousand men on that ship, and your father has their respect, and he has that respect because he is a fine disciplinarian. How would it look if his son, . . . showed up looking like a beatnik?" And when the haircut wasn't short enough (of course!) Dad had the ship's barber finish the job. Jim Morrison was a typical American kid in the 1960s. He had it all. But something was missing.

Jim himself discovered the absence, and started trying to fill it, at UCLA. He crammed notebooks with scribbling about the nature of film. He made an unscripted, surrealistic film about film that layered together shots of a friend's girlfriend in her undies standing on a TV full of Nazis with shots of Jim toking on a pot pipe. He made friends with one of his hip film teachers and then fell out with him when he gave him a *D* for his girlie/TV/Nazi/pot movie. He was exhibitionistic and moody and was accused of being a dilettante. He got drunk and goofed around.

He met Ray Manzarek and dropped out of school to join the burgeoning hippie scene in the sleazy beach area of Venice. He became interested in starting a band, even though he had never before been interested in music and could neither sing (as such things are conventionally judged) nor play an instrument. He also wanted to join the burgeoning music scene that was at the center (which Jim had *always* been interested in) of that hippie scene. He wrote some poem-songs. He met Ray Manzarek again.

On the Venice beach, after some small talk, Jim squatted in the sand and recited to Ray the first verse of "Moonlight Drive." Said Ray, "Those are the greatest fuckin' song lyrics I've ever heard. Let's start a rock 'n' roll band and make a million dollars."

Said Jim: "Exactly. That's what I had in mind all along."

Ray was a trained musician playing in a semisuccessful semipro group that already had a contract with a small local label. Ray brought Jim into the band and, despite his cohorts skepticism, put music to Jim's lyrics and tried to help Jim become a singer. As the other musicians gradually drifted away, Ray recruited a more simpatico pair, drummer John Densmore and guitarist Robby Krieger, and when he couldn't find a suitable bass player, he decided to double on keyboard bass himself. The band was complete, and Jim named them the Doors. They promptly went out and failed to make a million dollars.

Nevertheless, Jim was busy, if not contented, opening plenty of other doors in his quest for the missing element in it all. More often than not, what Jim found on the other side of those doors was a mirror, and his own reflection. Or, as he put it in "When the Music's Over": "The face in the mirror won't stop." A female friend who used to let Morrison stay at her apartment when he was too fucked up to make it back to Venice recalled coming home frequently to find him "posing in front of the mirror, sucking in his cheeks like a fashion model with the haunting, hungry *Vogue* magazine look, preening his still-damp hair." She also recalled how for the six months they were friendly, Jim Morrison never spoke louder than a whisper—and how she finally got sick of it.

"What is this bullshit?" she yelled at him one day. "You don't *really* talk that way. Now stop it."

When Morrison then tried to regain the upper hand by seducing her, she became totally fed up. "Don't be such a goddamned phony," she said, in what was no doubt the most cutting insult one could hurl at a young poseur like Morrison.

Jim responded by grabbing a knife from the kitchen, putting his friend in a hammerlock, and pressing the blade at her midsection. "You can't say that to me," he said. "I'm gonna cut you and see if you bleed." She *hoped* he was acting this time. A moment later, the scene was interrupted by the arrival of John Densmore, and Jim laughed it all off.

Another door Jim Morrison opened—again and again—was drugs. Behind this door he found a fun-house mirror. But while it may have been funny to Jim, sometimes it wasn't so funny to his friends. Drummer Densmore, whom Manzarek had discovered in a meditation class, found it downright infuriating in the struggling early days of 1966.

After a brief brush with glory, when Columbia Records signed and then a few months later dropped them, the band slid steadily downward. On the rare occasion when they played outside their dingy rehearsal space, promoters and the public were generally hostile. But after a friend wangled an audition for them and they packed the house with other cheering friends, they had their first steady club gig at the Whiskey A Go Go in the heart of the L.A. action. Although they were fired and rehired by the owner practically every week, they slowly but surely began to build up a real following, and Elektra Records decided to take a chance on them. Their luck had begun to turn again. They were beginning to *make* it. And Jim's behavior—the same outrageous behavior that had gotten them attention in the first place—was threatening to blow it all away. Jim was failing to draw the proper line between life and art, between business and pleasure.

Densmore complained to Manzarek about Jim's drug taking and the resultant erratic behavior while they raced over to their lead singer's apartment to investigate the latest instance of that behavior, specifically to find out why he had yet to show up for that evening's Whiskey performance. Counseling tolerance, Manzarek reminded Densmore that the drummer, too, had once been a drug taker. Replied John, unmollified: "I never took acid more than once a week, and Jim's on it every other day, at least."

The two of them knocked on Morrison's door and pleaded with him to come out. A pregnant pause. The door swung open. Jim Morrison stared out. "Ten thousand mikes," he said. And they knew what he meant, even though they couldn't quite believe it. A normal dose of acid is closer to 300 micrograms.

While the next set back at the club was a mess, according to Danny Sugarman and Jerry Hopkins, in their Morrison biography, *No One Here Gets Out Alive,* Morrison made a great breakthrough in the final one. He reinvented a song about faded love called "The End"—the apocalyptic, Oedipal epic that sealed his special fame. The authors are suggesting that the song sprang directly from the evening's acid experience. Jim's Dionysian genius was supposedly bigger and stronger than even the strongest dose of acid. Jim could ride "the snake," as he would call it, of LSD overdose and make it work for him. In all probability, the authors' sources within the band are engaging in 20/20 hindsight as well as a bit of hero worship and legend mongering, unconscious though it might be. The version of "The End" that night was probably neither so polished nor so unrehearsed. It's a good story and in line with the reverent tone of the text, but if it's true, it's probably a momentary aberration. Although Morrison's drug abuse may have resulted in some inspired moments, mostly it just killed him.

In late 1966, the Doors recorded their first album for Elektra. During the sessions, a drunken Jim sprayed a fire extinguisher all over the control board and didn't remember it the next day. Elektra indulgently picked up the damages. The LP was released in January 1967, and its first single was a tune called "Break on Through."

In the same vein as that title, the press kit for the new group included these autobiographical notes by Morrison: "You could say it's an accident that I was ideally suited for the work I am doing; it's the feeling of a bowstring being pulled back for 22 years and suddenly let go. I am primarily an American; second, a Californian; third, a Los Angeles resident. I've always been attracted to ideas that were about revolt against authority. When you make your peace with authority you become an authority. I like ideas about the breaking away or overthrowing of established order. I am interested in anything about revolt, disorder, chaos, especially activity that seems to have no meaning." He also made a point of noting in his personal data that his parents were dead— when in fact they were only so in Jim's mind.

The Doors juggernaut rolled slowly up and down California and then across the country. "Break on Through" became a minor hit in L.A., but in June they released as their second single an edited version of another tune from the album, "Light My Fire." The critics went wild. So did the public. The band came to New York and triumphed. Critic Lillian Roxon, author of *The Rock Encyclopedia,* described them as "unendurable pleasure prolonged." By the first week in August, *Billboard,* the music-biz bible, listed their first album as number one in the nation. The Doors—and in particular their sex-symbol lead singer—were stars.

Because, in his imagination, his career was already well under way from the start, stardom didn't much change Jim. He had *always* been a star. Like Patti Smith, who would later emulate him, Jim Morrison lived in a fantasy world where he was already a great poet and philosopher, a latter-day Nietzsche or Rimbaud. Stardom just meant that other people now believed it, which was *their* problem. Quantitatively, stardom ensured that Jim would never lack for the booze, drugs, or squalid one-night stands that he imagined were not only his due as a rock 'n' roll star, but his duty as a great romantic artist. And it helped ensure that his fantasy bubble would never be broken by outsiders.

His parents were two of those outsiders. It wasn't until well after the release of the first Doors album that George and Clara Morrison became aware of their son's new career. Until a friend brought the album to the attention of their other son, Andy, all the Morrisons knew was that Jim had disappeared into the "beatnik" underground of L.A. with the vague notion of starting a rock band. After Andy played the record to Clara, she made a determined effort to reconnect with Jim, with whom she hadn't spoken for a year.

Through Elektra, she was able to reach him on the phone and

ask him, please, to come home for Thanksgiving. Then she added: "One thing, Jim. Will you do your mother a big favor? You know how your father is. Will you get a haircut before you come home?" When Jim had said good-bye and hung up, he turned to his factotums and stated: "I don't want to talk to her ever again." Thus, when she later tried to come backstage at a Doors show, his factotums deflected her. And in the end, he never saw or spoke to that particular balloon puncturer again.

Jim Morrison's fantasy balloon eventually rose high enough to attract a *lot* of would-be puncturers. It's hard to recall, but those were the last days of Lyndon Johnson and the first of the second coming of Richard Nixon. People thought that rock 'n' roll could actually change the world. And not all of the people who thought that were swelled-headed rock stars. One of them, who was merely a swelled-headed government worker, was J. Edgar Hoover, head of the FBI. He kept files on people like Morrison. Others may well have included the police department of New Haven, Connecticut, where the Doors arrived for a concert on December 9, 1968, the day after Jim Morrison turned twenty-four.

In 1968, it was practically illegal to dance at rock 'n' roll concerts, despite the fact that the basic point—before people like J. Edgar Hoover politicized it—was to dance. Rock 'n' roll, it now seems ludicrous to explain, is for moving and grooving, screaming and hollering and blowing off steam. As they did at the Doors concert that evening, as they did at rock concerts all over the country (though particularly at those featuring Morrison or Janis Joplin), cops lined the front of the stage. Not only couldn't the kids *dance,* they weren't even allowed to *stand* at their seats!

But the trouble in New Haven started before the show, backstage, where Jim was chatting up a local girl. Looking for a more intimate place to talk, Morrison located a shower stall. In a few minutes, he and the girl were making out. Suddenly, the door flew open and a cop, who evidently didn't recognize the star of the show, told them that no one was allowed backstage. Jim challenged the cop, who insisted. Finally, grabbing his own crotch, Morrison told the cop to "eat it!" The cop then drew his can of Mace and fired away. But that's just for openers.

A Doors functionary showed up, the cop realized his mistake, and the two washed out Jim's eyes. The cop also apologized. The recovered Morrison and the Doors hit the stage. But in the middle of "Back Door Man," Jim started telling the audience what had happened backstage. He spoke in terms that today hardly seem so inflammatory, terms that in any case were well within his First Amendment rights.

As one by one the cops at the front of the stage began to turn around and glower, Jim recounted how he and the girl "wanted some privacy. . . . And so we went into this shower room. We weren't doing anything, you know. Just standing there and talking. . . . And then this little man came in there, this little man in a little blue suit and a little blue cap. . . . " Jim depicted the cop as a redneck moron, concluding: " . . . And then he reached 'round behind him and he brought out this little black can of somethin'. Looked like shaving cream. And then he sprayed it in my eyes."

Leading back into "Back Door Man," Morrison shouted: "The whole world hates me! . . . The whole fucking world hates me." And then the lights went on. Warned that the constabulary was up in arms, Jim nevertheless persisted, yelling, "Turn off the lights!" At that moment, a police lieutenant walked onstage and arrested Jim Morrison, who in a final act of defiance held out the microphone, saying: "Okay, pig, come on, say your thing, man!"

The cops tossed Morrison and a roadie into the squad car. At the jail, where he was booked for "an indecent and immoral exhibition," disturbing the peace, and resisting arrest, they taunted him about being a long-haired pretty boy and he taunted back that they were ugly. One cop promised to take care of Morrison when he got off duty at midnight, but fortunately the Doors' manager arrived with bail in time. The charges were not terribly serious, and eventually Morrison got off.

But the arrest meant nervous promoters, lost gigs, and angry cops—not to mention the possibility that some vindictive right-wing judge would decide to make Morrison an example to the other rebellious youth of the nation and send him off to do time. That was a very real possibility in those days.

By this time, the Doors had released two best-selling and critically well-received albums. But for Jim, something was still missing. His quest for the missing element in it all, his search for love and meaning, had begun to create its own void, and everything around it was being sucked in. The third album, a mess from the start, was turning into a pretentious, messy bore.

So was Morrison, but with an uglier twist. He was picking up young girls on Sunset Strip, abusing them verbally and sexually, "buttfucking" them, and discarding them like the empty beer cans that littered the ten-bucks-a-night motel rooms he seemed to prefer to his Topanga Canyon home.

Common-law wife Pamela Courson did not fare much better than the groupies he flaunted before her. Eventually she took solace in heroin—and then helped ensnare Jim. Morrison even abused his fellow rock stars, grabbing Janis Joplin by the hair at a party and shoving her face into his crotch until she escaped, weeping. When she returned, as Morrison was leaving, she began beating him over the head with a bottle of Southern Comfort. He laughed. Morrison goofed off and threw money around on expensive rock-star clothing and indulged himself in all ways imaginable, but mostly through this period, he drank. All day. All night.

When they saw him lying in a puddle of his own piss on the studio floor—after causing John Densmore to quit the band in utter disgust—Ray Manzarek and Robby Krieger decided to seek help. They eventually enlisted the man who had previously been enlisted to curtail Janis Joplin's drinking: musician, Dylan crony, and self-described "hangout artist" Bobby Neuwirth. The effect on Jim was roughly the same as it had been on Janis. As Neuwirth himself said, "Let's face it, there wasn't no way to talk Jim outta havin' a drink. You just ended up having one with him." By most accounts, Neuwirth was a blast to be around. But he did not stop his clients from killing themselves. And so the Doors, rejoined by Densmore, staggered on.

Jim Morrison wanted to be a poet, a Rimbaud. Sometime in 1968 it began to dawn on him, through the haze, that he was a rock star. Jim Morrison was bursting his own bubble. One day he came into the Doors' offices and announced he was quitting. "It's not what I want to do," he said. Ray asked for, and got, six more months.

In the next six months, the Doors sold close to a million copies of their weak third album, *Waiting for the Sun* and a million of the bubble-gum single from it, "Hello, I Love You," which happened to be the first song Morrison ever wrote, back when he was exploring the possibilities in Venice. Inside the album was the text of Morrison's epic poem, "Celebration of the Lizard," which hadn't quite worked out as a song.

In the next six months, the Doors played their biggest, most prestigious concert dates ever. Following in the footsteps of the Beatles, they played the Hollywood Bowl and became the first band to graduate from the Fillmore to New York's Madison Square Garden. A second single from the LP, "Touch Me," also sold a million. Then the band conquered Europe, despite the fact that in Amsterdam they were forced to play as a trio, with Ray singing, when Jim passed out after eating a bunch of hash and had to be hospitalized. In the next six months, the Doors became bigger than ever, pulling down as much as $35,000 a night for crowds never numbering less than 10,000. Though the critics and older fans were beginning to abandon the Doors, hordes of teenyboppers who thought Morrison was a sex god were more than making up for it.

In the next six months, Jim Morrison also became sicker than ever of being a sex god and rock star, and he laid the groundwork for his escape. He delved back into film with a concert-fantasy called *Feast of Friends* and, through the poet Michael McClure, acquired an agent who would peddle his poems to book publishers. In early 1969, he attended a performance of the avant-garde Living Theater in which the actors stripped naked and shouted about freedom and ran through the audience, teasing and taunting, before they were promptly busted. Jim identified totally. In fact, his biographers say the performance changed

Morrison's life. Indeed, according to their thesis, it killed him.

Not literally, of course. The next day Morrison was drinking and carrying on all the way to Miami, where the Doors had a big concert scheduled for the night. In fact, Jim drank and carried on so much that he missed a connecting flight in New Orleans and had all that much more time to drink and carry on.

By the time he finally arrived in Miami, he was completely stewed, even for Morrison. It took the band 10 minutes to get his attention onstage, and then he would only get one or two verses into a song before breaking it off to rap—or drink. The band started many different songs, trying to draw him into *their* performance, but as it turned out, Jim had at some point ceased performing with the Doors and had joined the Living Theater, all by himself. First he harangued the audience, calling them "a bunch of slaves." Then he told them to make love to each other. Then he told them to make love to him. He tossed his shirt into the audience, and then he stuck his hand in the top of his pants. Ray could see what was, so to speak, coming, and before Morrison could get his dick out (or so says Ray), the keyboardist dispatched a roadie, who grabbed Jim by the waistband and prevented it.

Morrison went on to incite the audience to charge the stage, and eventually one of the promoter's henchmen literally heaved Jim off. Whereupon the resourceful drunk led a snake dance through the crowd and into the balcony and then somehow found his way back to the dressing room. What the concert may have lacked musically it compensated for theatrically, and everybody, supposedly even the cops, had a good time. According to plan, Morrison left the next day for a vacation in Jamaica. He should have stuck around for the reviews.

The newspapers started it, with reports of near riot, obscenity, and various other forms of mayhem. The politicians picked it up, raising a moral outcry that such a thing could happen in a city-owned auditorium. A Jesus teen organized an anti-obscenity rally. And the prosecutor went to work on a case. One week after the show, on March 5, 1969, with a public employee serving as complainant, the City of Miami issued a warrant for James

Morrison's arrest for a felony and three misdemeanors.

The felony was for "lewd and lascivious behavior," specifically that Morrison "did lewdly and lasciviously expose his penis, place his hands upon his penis and shake it, and further the said defendant did simulate the acts of masturbation upon himself and oral copulation upon another." Though they at first laughed off the possible seven-and-a-half-year sentence, the Doors soon realized that the charges had another, more immediate effect as promoters in droves began to cancel Doors dates all across the country. For the moment, the (arguably) biggest American band of its era was virtually unemployable.

The respite did give Jim a chance to work on his other art projects. For his new film, *HWY*, Jim wrote himself a scene in which, tethered by a safety rope, he did a little jig on an 18-inch ledge 17 stories above Sunset Boulevard. Predictably, but still to the horror of friends and film crew, he tossed away the tether during his dance and closed the act by pissing over the edge. At the same time, he self-published his two books of poems, *The Lords* and *The New Creatures* (later published in one volume by Simon & Schuster), in parchment-leaved, gilded editions that marked them unmistakably as vanity books paid for by a wealthy dilettante.

Jim also gave up his leather pants, grew a beard, performed on public television, and sat down for an in-depth *Rolling Stone* interview with Jerry Hopkins. During this interview the rock star admitted that his parents weren't dead and expounded on his life, art, and philosophy, included his drinking; which he described as "the difference between suicide and slow capitulation" and which he quite diligently maintained.

By this point, Jim Morrison probably didn't have much choice about the drinking. He was an addict and could no more go without his booze than a junkie could go without his heroin. And during this period the incidents precipitated by that compulsive drinking continued. Some of the incidents were almost amusing, as when he passed out on the couch after his twenty-fifth birthday party at his manager's and while still comatose managed to extract his dick and begin peeing on the carpet. The manager rushed over with a bucket brigade of wine goblets, and Morrison filled three full.

Other drunken incidents were not funny at all. One of those occurred when Jim and a buddy decided on a whim to take in a Rolling Stones concert in Phoenix, an hour's flight away. Following the consumption en route to the airport of a six-pack and a bottle of Courvoisier, the two boarded a commercial jet and began throwing food and harassing the stewardess. Ignoring a warning by the captain, they found themselves hauled off in handcuffs when the plane hit the tarmac in Arizona, where they would spend the next 36 hours in jail. They were charged—by the FBI, no less—under a provision of the new skyjacking law and, if convicted, faced 10 years in the federal pen.

Jim also married during this time, but not Pam (who was never more than his common-law wife, if that, although she called herself Pam Morrison). It wasn't exactly a bride-wore-white wedding. It was a witch ceremony, performed by a high priestess of a coven, in which bride and groom drank each other's blood and stepped over a broomstick and signed in blood a marriage certificate made out in witch runes. The bride was editor of a rock magazine, and though she eventually turned up pregnant (subsequently aborted), the union was evidently no more serious than a lot of things drunks do so seriously.

The last time his witch wife saw him was at the end of a long day of tequila. "He looked waxen, rigid—horrible," she recalled. "He looked already dead, lying there with the couch framing him like a coffin. I knew then I'd never see him alive again."

The next day Jim flew with Pamela to Paris, where, as drunks also do, he came down with pneumonia. He recovered, of course. He always recovered. As someone once said about drugs, everyone handles them so well—until he doesn't. Morrison had amazing powers of recovery, wrote Hopkins and Sugerman. Until he didn't.

"Does anyone believe in omens?" asked Jim Morrison when he read that Jimi Hendrix had died. He was standing outside a Miami courtroom where closing arguments were about to be heard in his overexposure trial. The judge was more or less railroading him. The outlook was bleak. But when the verdict came in, the jury had let him off on the more serious lewd-behavior felony, while convicting him only of misdemeanor exposure. It was far from the worst verdict. Nevertheless, a month later the judge sentenced him to the max: six months in jail. The sentence stunned and depressed Jim, although he remained free on bail pending appeal. And then he got back to L.A. and word arrived that Janis Joplin had died. Omens? Apparently Jim believed in them. To friends he began to brag drunkenly, "You're drinking with number three." Thing is, they were.

Jim told *Circus* magazine he really had no regrets. However, he said, "If I had it to do over... I think I would have gone for the quiet, demonstrative artist-plodding-away-in-his-own-garden trip." No doubt with such a thought in mind, Jim made vague plans to return to Paris, which had enchanted him. While he had sworn off concertizing in the aftermath of Miami, he now agreed to a few dates—two, to be precise. Even following the unexpected critical success of the new *Morrison Hotel* LP, two dates were all the band could get any promoter to book.

The first, by most accounts, went great. At the second, in New Orleans, Ray Manzarek saw Morrison's spirit go. "He lost all his energy about midway through the set. He hung on the microphone and it just slipped away." After New Orleans, Morrison never again performed live with the Doors. He completed the next album, *L.A. Woman,* which followed a live LP and a greatest-hits collection and fulfilled the Doors', contractual obligation to Elektra. Jim knew that the Miami appeal might go on forever, but due to a last-minute recant of testimony, he had gotten off on the Phoenix charges. With his house in order, or as much as it might ever be, Morrison firmed up his escape to France to salvage a dream.

Whatever Jim had hoped to accomplish in Paris was rapidly drowned in a sea of booze. In addition to the coke he had been snorting on and off for about a year, he now added the occasional blast of heroin, copped at a Paris disco that had become a trendy

junkie hangout. After three months of such activity, Jim slid into
a massive depression. Perhaps he was also unhappy about the
quality of his recent writing, his Parisian poetry. Perhaps he was
in retrospect disappointed in the writing he had done for his two
earlier books, which had just been released in paperback by
Simon & Schuster.

The friends who invited him to dinner that Friday, July 2,
1971, found him more or less inconsolable. After dinner, one
story goes, he took Pamela home and went to the movies. After
dinner, another story goes, he and Pam went home together.
Whatever the case, sometime in the 12 hours that followed
dinner, the body of Jim Morrison got into a bathtub in his rented
flat and never got out.

A friend of mine who accompanied Jim through several of his
final days says it was pretty definitely heroin, not a heart attack,
as was reported to the press, that killed the erstwhile Lizard King
and Rimbaud manqué. My friend told me this several years ago,
before the Hopkins–Sugerman bio came out, when some of us
still pretty much believed the official story, when we still pretty
much believed official stories in general, when we were all a lot
younger. They found Jim in the bathtub because that's the kind of
thing you do with heroin ODs to try to revive them. Cold water,
slaps in the face. Wife (so to speak) Pam, no stranger to the H-
drug herself, and maybe some unidentified friend—*definitely*
some unidentified friend, considering how much Jim weighed
from all those years of drinking—dragged him to the tub. But it
was too late. Maybe this shot was just the final, self-destructive
straw that broke Jim Morrison's back—or liver. Maybe he got a
hot shot, a dose of near-pure shit, maybe from that heroin-soaked
Rock 'n' Roll Circus nightclub where he'd taken to hanging out.
Yeah, maybe some low-rent Mafia dealer wanted the thrill of
knowing, and inevitably saying, that he'd offed the world-
famous lead singer of the Doors. Or maybe some fan was trying
to give him a treat. Or maybe it was an accident—even *junkies*
have accidents, you know. In any event, it was heroin, says my
friend.

There's a great Jim Morrison quote from an article in the old

L.A. Free Press. It's about booze. "I know people drink because they're bored," he said. "But I enjoy drinking. It loosens people up and stimulates conversation sometimes. And, uh, it's, I don't know, it's like gambling somehow. You know? You go out for a night of drinking and you don't know where you're going to end up the next day. It could work out good and it could be disastrous. It's like a throw of the dice."

His body was laid to rest in Père-Lachaise, the graveyard of Chopin . . . and Rimbaud. Fifteen years later a new generation of teenyboppers thinks that's exactly where Jim Morrison's body belongs—that is, if he's truly dead. The official cause of death was a heart attack. More accurately, Jim Morrison just finally crapped out.

10

JANIS JOPLIN

American Crosses

I met Janis Joplin once. I was standing by the door of the Different Drummer on Lexington Avenue, around 1968. I was sifting through a $2 bin full of last year's tie-dyed haberdashery, and in she walked, her highness the queen of the hippies. Smiled at me, my face not two feet from hers, and then scrooched on by. It was puffy, the face. No, make that bloated. Make that swollen. A sad, mad face that had been buffed and sanded to an unhealthy pink rubber-ball sheen and still festered with pimples. Not to mention that she was short, stubby-legged, and sometimes overweight, and had this ratty, frizzy hair.

And yet—look at the photographs—there was something oddly attractive about her. I remember seeing her do her thing down at the Fillmore and nearly messing my pants. From the back row, the girl from Port Arthur cut a pretty mean figure, in miniskirt and spangles and feathers. And I always *loved* the way she parted her hair just a little bit off the center and how it fell down across one eye in a wavy cascade. And those eyes! Most brilliant blue, and shining out like a laser blast from under sultrily dropped lids, beneath achingly knitted brows. And her voice—with one full-bore phrase it could have blown down the doors to Fort Knox, and then on a tune like "Mercedes Benz," send Mr. T searching for his hanky! She was beautiful and sexy. And she was ugly, too. But perhaps her greatest trick was that for a moment, when she sang, she was neither. And neither, for a moment, were we.

There are some things about the hippie days that you have to miss. One of them was the breaking down of the esthetic monolith and the pluralization of beauty. A whole generation of frizzy-haired girls were freed from the secret Friday-evening ritual of ironing their hair, just as a whole generation of Afro-Americans was freed by the sixties from having to use lye on *their* hair. A whole generation of non-Nordic girls and boys was given back its dignity, restored to its *own* beauty. And then there are some things about the hippie days you don't have to miss at all. There was, along with that inclusiveness, an unmistakable exclusiveness—in other words, a frizzy-haired girl was cool, but only so long as she was also a hippie. That brings up another not-so-cool sixties thing: To be a hippie meant adhering to certain alternate conventions of dress and behavior no less rigid than those of straight society. Which brings up still other things: One of those behaviors was promiscuous sex; another was drug taking. Janis Joplin embodied those, too. She was, at the same time, the very good and the very bad of those days.

Janis Joplin never had a prayer. She could never be part of the majority because Janis Joplin—and this fact runs through her life like a mainline of barium on an X-ray plate—was deemed ugly. Zitty, frizzy, dumpy, and *ugly*. And while we all have our own crosses, God help the ugly broads. In our Miss America culture, their's is surely the hardest to bear.

Myra Friedman, her publicist, friend, and biographer, has described Janis's adolescent weight problem and the skin condition that went "far beyond anything that could be termed a teenager's siege of acne." She also has described her classmates' reaction to Janis: "The students threw things at her, they mocked her, they called her names, of which 'pig' was the favorite." But that's not the half of it, as Friedman details, nor the worst. In the winter of 1962, having finally turned her back on the provincial ugliness that was Port Arthur and made her way to sophisticated Austin in the Texas foothills, she got herself some good gigs—

and reviews—singing in the Austin folk clubs, and began classes at UT. Just when she seemed to have made good her escape, Janis Joplin was visited by an awful specter. "Janis was publicly pilloried for the benefit of the entire student body at the University of Texas," writes Friedman, "nominated for the lofty position of Ugliest Man on Campus."

Like so many American misfits and rejects before her, Janis Joplin headed for land's end, to San Francisco, about as far from Port Arthur as she could go without a visa. Urged to make the trip by her friend Chet Helms, a Haight-Ashbury founding father and a mover in what was left of the beatnik scene, Janis quickly found singing work in the coffeehouses and the tolerant welcome she had never before known. She also found a mode of escape that didn't require a visa or travel, and she employed it with abandon. Indeed, as she told author David Dalton, "I wanted to smoke dope, take dope, lick dope, suck dope, fuck dope, anything I could lay my hands on I wanted to do it. . . . Hey, man, what is it? I'll try it. How do you do it? Do you suck it? No? You swallow it? I'll swallow it." Mostly she did speed and booze, with some pot thrown in. Some say she also did heroin, but most agree that came later. In any case, could anyone really blame her?

"You mentioned the Ugliest Man incident," says Myra Friedman in conversation today, "and I don't think there's any doubt that was one of the more brutal acts of adolescent cruelty to a peer and really quite devastating. But it's not so simple, that she was not attractive and therefore they did not like her. The most popular gal in my high school was definitely not the most beautiful—as a matter of fact, she was not very attractive at all. Janis, you see, also cultivated certain kinds of negative things. She was a very confused and troubled adolescent, for reasons that we'll probably never know fully. Because they are naturally protective of their child and their privacy, the interaction between the Joplins and Janis has never been made entirely clear. Which is not to say that the Joplins are not very fine and good people, which they are. And Janis was certainly not an abused child. . . . More a mixture between spoiled—and a very strong mother."

Long before San Francisco, in other words, or even Austin, somewhere deep in the heart of Port Arthur, Texas, Janis Joplin had somehow been emotionally perverted. As nice as it was, the welcome she found in San Francisco came too late, which is why in many quarters that welcome was eventually withdrawn.

If her familiarity with heroin came later, her familiarity with needles arrived with the speed. Already a user in San Francisco, Janis spent most of her summer 1964 trip to New York speeding: yammering at her yammering speedfreak friends, yammering at the walls, at the floor, at the cockroaches that ruled in the Lower East Side tenement. She also learned to be more efficient with her speed by shooting it. She also overcame the fear of the needle that helps keep so many away from a mainline drug habit; she developed a skill with the spike that would later lead her girlfriend Peggy to describe her as an "artist" of the needle, hitting first time every time. She began the dealing that would continue in the fall upon her return to San Francisco and that helped her make the rent money and, mainly, her own increasing methamphetamine bills. Janis had become totally ensnared. Back on the West Coast, she tried to commit herself to San Francisco General to make herself stop, but she was turned away as some sort of welfare cheat. She warned a visiting friend—and she wasn't just bragging—"Don't let anybody ever get near you with a needle!" Finally, in the summer of 1965, having degenerated into "a vegetable, an 88-pound spastic speedfreak," as friends recalled it for biographer Friedman, Janis even returned to Port Arthur to get away from it.

Needless to say, although she did quit speed, Port Arthur didn't work out in the long run, nor did wearing her hair in a neat bun and putting on a modest dress and attending the local college. Within a few months, presumably healthy again, she began to sing around in the Houston folk scene. But where the audience expected Joan Baez, she gave them Bessie Smith, and so singing didn't quite work out either. By the following May, 1966, she had returned to Austin, where at least they appreciated her voice and where she had been invited to join Roky Erikson's Thirteenth Floor Elevators. When the last didn't quite work out and Chet

Helms invited her back to San Francisco, a new scene, and a new band he was assembling, Janis split Texas for good. She arrived at Helms's door on June 4, 1966.

Helms called the band Big Brother and the Holding Company. He was the manager. Conveniently, he was also the manager of the Avalon Ballroom, where Big Brother and the Holding Company made their debut on June 10, 1966. Reaction was mixed. First, Janis didn't know how to play in front of a rock band. Second, the guys in the rock band didn't know how to play, period. But working together—and then living together in the tiny town of Lagunitas in rural western Marin County—things gradually began to come together. The sound began to work, and so did the look, inspired by James Gurley's stylishly avant-garde wife, Nancy. Soon enough, Janis had shucked her masculine shirts for lace, velvet, beads, and feathers enough to choke a gypsy queen. After she traveled to the newly opened Fillmore auditorium and checked out the high-voltage Otis Redding—she stood at the edge of the stage through every set so as not to miss a trick—the final missing piece fell into place and the new Janis Joplin was complete.

"They wanted to see her shoot up, they wanted to see her get loud, they wanted to see her scream and yell and screech about," Country Joe McDonald, who lived with Janis for three or four months during this period, said after her death. "I don't know what happened to her in Texas in her childhood, but I got the feeling that she was just the wrong person in the wrong place and got treated in the wrong way."

When Chet Helms found he no longer had time to direct the affairs of both Big Brother and the Avalon Ballroom, the band sought a new manager. Returning from a four-week gig in Chicago, where, after not being paid in full, they had been lured into the kind of independent record contract that traditionally makes for trouble when the major labels come around, they certainly needed a manager. They hired an idealistic, relatively inexperienced local boy named Julius Karpen, whose first, and perhaps most important, suggestion was that the band move back into the city. Back in S.F., Janis started living with Country Joe, and Big Brother became inextricably bound up with the Haight-Ashbury scene that in January 1967 was poised to explode out of San Francisco and into the nation's consciousness. The Jefferson Airplane, Country Joe and the Fish, the Grateful Dead, and Big Brother and the Holding Company: In the months ahead they would become the stars of a scene that would vainly profess to have none.

The explosion came in two parts, like an atom bomb: first, the local, more conventional explosion that drives the atoms toward each other, and then the second, all-encompassing blast when the atoms collide. The local explosion came in June 1967, right down the peninsula from San Francisco, in a pretty little seaside town. It was the Monterey Pop Festival, and when the dust had settled, it had catalyzed a human swarming phenomenon in San Francisco known as the Summer of Love that still reverberates today and had catapulted several new names into the pop-culture firmament: among them, Janis Joplin. Within five months of Monterey, Julius Karpen was out as manager and Albert Grossman, the big-league hardballer who managed Bob Dylan and other top acts, was in; Big Brother and the Holding Company had reportedly signed an unprecedented lucrative contract with Columbia Records, while some of the original San Francisco hippies held a Death of Hippie funeral march through their now overrun Haight—partly in honor of the fact that their beloved homegrown hippie bands had recently been featured on the cover of the straight world's loathsome *Life* magazine. Nevertheless, if the hippie scene was undergoing a frantic cooptation, Janis Joplin had at last "attained acceptance," writes Myra Friedman. "She had trimmed down to a slight and attractive figure. She had acquired the aura, which, while not of a conventional beauty, had the irresistible radiance of energy. No longer an outcast, at twenty-four she was a queen. . . . "

Big Brother was a great bad band, not unlike the Grateful Dead. Technically unaccomplished, they still managed to project a raw energy that was, in fact, the essence of the Haight-Ashbury musical esthetic. They were inspired amateurs, and—beyond the fact that they thus perfectly suited the tribal milieu in which they circulated—Big Brother accomplished musical things by accident, through ignorance, that would not occur to accomplished players. This fact escaped Columbia Records. Columbia, in the person of its illustrious president Clive Davis, seemed to see only Janis Joplin the solo artist, as did, it soon become apparent, Grossman. Their plans, unstated perhaps, perhaps understood, were to eventually free Janis from these woolly mammoth accompanists and allow her to achieve *true* greatness.

This basic misunderstanding of the nature of the band caused many of the difficulties in recording the first album. John Simon, the producer assigned by Columbia, was fairly well horrified at the band's ability in the studio. Hoping to salvage the project and perhaps capture some of what the concert-going public appreciated, as well as to cover up some of their deficiencies, he arranged to record the LP live, more or less (in many instances, the "liveness" was actually simulated in the studio). It turned out to be the right decision for the wrong reasons. *Cheap Thrills,* as the album was titled—shortened from Janis's suggestion of *Sex, Dope & Cheap Thrills*—turned out to be a pumping powerhouse of a record. And funky Big Brother was the perfect setting for the powerhouse singing of Janis Joplin, who after all *wasn't* Billie Holliday or Bessie Smith or Big Mama Thornton or, for that matter, Tina Turner or Otis Redding. Joined with Big Brother, Janis's unrefined, derivative style brought the blues together with psychedelic space music and pounding rock 'n' roll in unpredictable, ever-shifting permutations. Stripped from Big Brother, it would run the risk of being merely ersatz.

In what was a harbinger of things to come, Janis called Myra Friedman during the recording sessions and, writes the former publicist, "demanded that I publicize a fight she'd had with Jim Morrison." Naturally, in Janis's telling, Jim was the vanquished. Honing the image of herself that would be etched in the history of the counterculture era, Janis at the same time was beginning to act like the old image of the Hollywood star, slavishly courting publicity and lashing out at subordinates. "But I must insist to you," says Myra Friedman today, "that it never went on when Janis was sober. I never heard Janis act like that when she wasn't on something. The only problem is, there wasn't a helluva lot of time when Janis wasn't on something. If she was off the dope, she was on the booze.''

Within months of the release of *Cheap Thrills,* it was announced that Big Brother and Janis would go their separate ways. That the move was a mistake became apparent quite rapidly. First, Janis was called to task in the rock and underground press for careerism, a dirty word in and of itself, but especially in connection with rock 'n' roll, especially *San Francisco* rock 'n' roll. Rock 'n' roll, since the Beatles, was supposed to be about the communal experience, like *Hard Day's Night.* Second, the band she assembled (with Sam Andrew the lone holdover from BB) was lame, as ersatz as they come—fake soul, fake blues played by faceless, soulless, subhacks (save, of course, Sam). Third, Janis's attempts to run things brought out the worst in that bad band, the worst in herself, both onstage and off, and were mostly laughable, according to those present. But she had her name above the title, and that was all that seemed to matter. Hey, Port Arthur, lookit me now!

What Port Arthur didn't see was that Janis's drinking had gotten much worse, to the point where, as much as the feather boa, a pint of Southern Comfort had become her emblem. This fact moved the Southern Comfort distillers (with some prodding from the prima donna herself) to fork over a $2,500 lynx coat by way of thanks for the publicity (which amused Janis no end). What Port Arthur also didn't see was that Janis had quite enthusiastically and openly taken to heroin. The third thing they didn't see was her homosexuality.

Janis's first gay experience apparently occurred during high school. There were more in Austin. And then, in the, so to speak, heady atmosphere of San Francisco in the Summer of Love, more girls still, sometimes in combination with boys. The lesbian and heroin-addicted portion of Janis's life is well-covered in an as-told-to book by one of her junkie lovers, Peggy Caserta. Entitled, with no little subtlety, *Going Down with Janis,* the book begins with the following characteristic sentence: "I was stark naked, stoned out of my mind on heroin, and the girl lying between my legs giving me head was Janis Joplin." It goes on: "It was not the first time we'd balled each other. . . . In three of the four years since I'd first met her in 1966, there had been so many times I couldn't keep track of them any longer. More often just the two of us; sometimes with one man between us, sometimes with two; sometimes before, wedged into, or after a succession of guys she'd fucked during a single day." It paints a scene of "numberless sets of sheets and countless tens of thousands of dollars' worth of dope [in] all the seedy and posh hotels, [in] the drive-ins, my boutique, New York, Philadelphia, Nashville, L.A., and Woodstock. . . . " It describes Janis Joplin coming and puking and shooting up and drinking. It details precisely how many fingers belonging to whom were used in what way and where. And it goes on and on, quickly becoming, after a few guilty hard-ons, unreadably boring. Probably the best of the book's good parts is the scene in the Woodstock Holiday Inn the day before the festival. Peggy arrives at the motel to find Janis already abed, with a guy. No problem—Janis makes some perfunctory apology and the dude is out on his ass, pants in hand.

" 'Oh, *baby,*' she whispered, ferrying me toward the bed and undressing me as she did. 'I'm so happy you're here.'

"I was exhausted, but the smack we immediately shot up lifted me above that on its warm wings. Less than ten minutes after Mitchell had pulled his cock out of her, we were arranged in the sixty-nine position and doing enough to one another with our respective mouths and fingers to go off, each of us, twice in the first half hour. . . . She moaned and screamed, tearing at my hair and rolling left and right until finally she went off the bed headfirst onto the rug. Pulling her up, I did all the rest of it with my mouth, worked up to a pitch myself by the knowledge that she'd sent Mitchell away so she could play with me. I couldn't bring myself to feel sorry for him. After a few moments at her soft fur it was obvious that he'd come in her at least once before I'd arrived. Now, as the walls of her vagina contracted in a final, orgasmic spasm and she expelled another dollop of his sperm, I lapped it up. Mixed with Janis' juices and stirred to the consistency of a soft sweet, it couldn't have tasted better if it were a spoonful of Baskin-Robbins Nutty Coconut ice cream."

That is, if you go for Nutty Coconut.

But even in the Caserta confessional, the depth of sadness in Janis's life will occasionally show through the prurience, as in the following exchange between the lovers:

"'Do you know what they used to call me in high school?' Janis said once, almost crying when she thought of it. '*Pig face!* Can you *imagine* what that does to a kid that young? I couldn't even get a date to my senior prom. It got to be two or three days before the prom, and finally my dad said he'd take me. But I wouldn't let him. I wouldn't give those bastards the satisfaction of seeing me there without a date.'"

In the meantime, though the new Kozmic Blues Band was a musical and sociological mistake, Janis Joplin was more in demand across the country than ever and, through the hard-bargaining Grossman, commanded amounts that escalated over the months from $20,000 to $30,000 to $50,000 and more for an appearance. Janis bought a beautiful house in the redwoods in the Marin County town of Larkspur and tooled around in a psyche-delically hand-painted Porsche. She scooped up clothing and scarfed down drinks and drugs and generally began to spin further off into space. Like Jim Morrison, and not too long after him, Janis—drunk, of course—was busted in Florida at the end of 1969 for profanity. It was a nothing incident, the kind of swearing you would later hear on the Nixon tapes. Janis was merely—and rightfully—enraged when a cop with a bullhorn came onstage during "Summertime" to try to bring order to the crowd. Of course, the crowd was not that disorderly to begin with—by today's standards, not at all—and the cop actually provoked them. So a shitfaced Janis got mad and cussed him out. A small fine was paid and she laughed it off, until, as had happened to Morrison and the Doors, nervous promoters across the country started calling off shows. For a time, Janis and her buddy Jim were the two top rock 'n' roll bad guys in the country, in the eyes of the authorities. While it gave them added chachet, it also lost them promotionally vital bookings. It also removed them from the one remotely constructive thing either was still capable of.

Finally, even Janis noticed her own fatal spin and sought professional help. "Dr. Rothschild," says Myra Friedman, "pointed out to her that she seemed to shoot up at the very moments when she would want to enjoy the experience. One of the effects of heroin on Janis was to deaden all feeling. She did not enjoy her moments of great triumph, so she'd go get stoned. There also seems to be some relation to the sexual behavior too, what heroin does in that regard. So she was going around deadening all the good stuff, as well as the bad stuff."

At the doctor's suggestion, Janis tried to kick with methadone. But that proved a short-lived experiment, and the spin was on again. Her drunk and stoned behavior one night on the phone was indicative of her state at this time. Calling Nashville for who knows what reason, she yelled at the operator: "This is Janis Joplin, J-O-P-L-I-N! I wanna speak to Johnny Cash! Just get him on the phone! I'm the biggest singer in America, you stupid nut, and he'll know who I am!" And surely he did. In the winter of 1969, *everyone* did: Janis Joplin was appearing on the cover of *Newsweek* magazine. Hey, Port Arthur, lookit me *now!*

Even as the spin turned into her final approach, Janis never forgot where she came from. And if her physical appearance wasn't her heaviest burden in life, it was close. "She was always talking about how ugly she was," said one lover from this time. "She'd say how in school they thought she was just an ugly girl of no significance, ugly and loud. I always had the impression that what she wanted to do was to go back to Port Arthur and be accepted and it didn't matter what she had to do to get that."

Suddenly that winter, Janis Joplin fell in love, for real, and kicked junk and, say her friends, got much better. Temporarily. A virtually nonstop, three-week party, with Kris Kristofferson and Bobby Neuwirth, at the Larkspur house, which climaxed in a virtual orgy in honor of Michael J. Pollard, promptly erased any impression of reform.

In the midst of all this, mostly through the help of Nick Gravenites and Mike Bloomfield, Janis managed to get together a new band that she called Full Tilt Boogie. Their first gig was at a Hell's Angels party in Marin. Though she had lately become disenchanted with the motorcycle outlaws, Janis was scared not to play. During the evening she got very drunk and got in a fight with an Angel mama, but remembered none of it the next day, neither the fight nor the playing. Even she was frightened.

If the omens seemed bad for Full Tilt Boogie, the omens were wrong. After its rocky start, the band turned out to be Janis's most complementary unit since Big Brother, while at the same time moving in the soul direction that Janis preferred. The posthumously released third album, *Pearl,* arguably her best, proves that. But if she was beginning to catch fire again artistically, it may have just meant that, like so many of these terminal cases, she was entering her burns-brightest phase, and it was now perhaps inevitable that she would soon expire.

Janis Joplin quit junk and started again. She cut back on her drinking and then increased it. She slept with one guy and then, by her own bragging, with 65 on a music-festival train traversing Canada. Her singing improved with the improvement in her band, gaining nuances it had never had before, but her career suffered the doldrums, partly due to nervous, inept promoters, partly due to a nascent disinterest in the R. Crumb cartoon character that Janis had finally become. "Well, I have to go change into Janis Joplin," she wearily told some friends backstage before one Full Tilt concert. "She's upstairs in a box!" And then, with the media playing it up as a great triumph, she decided to go home for her tenth high school reunion in Port Arthur and there carried on in more or less typical fashion. In an ultimately cruel remark that would surely cause Janis Joplin to roll over in her grave, one Port Arthur woman commented afterward: "They called her a 'pig' in high school; they were calling her a 'pig' at the end."

It wasn't long before Janis's ups and downs became simply down, down, downs. After all, she was dying. Chet Helms said that when she kissed him mockingly one evening toward the end, her face looked like a "vision from *Naked Lunch.*" Myra Friedman recalls Janis's face at their last encounter as being marked by "haunted eyes" and a "pulpy swell" with a "weird sickly pink" cast.

She was down in Los Angeles recording *Pearl,* and it was going well. She complained to Myra Friedman that her new and very serious boyfriend, Seth Morgan, was not coming to visit enough, but otherwise she didn't appear remarkably unhappy. Though she was staying in the Landmark Hotel, her old junkie hangout, there was no evidence that she had gone back to junk, nor that she had hooked up again with her junkie girlfriend Peggy Caserta. But by sometime around the middle of September she had done both. On September 18, Hendrix died. At the request of the AP, Myra called for a quotable comment. "Oh, I dunno," said Janis, "I was just thinking . . . I wonder what they'll say about *me* after I die." She commented similarly to others, but likely it was just a bit of romantic self-indulgence. Eventually, several people found out she was back on heroin. They begged her to stop. But their efforts were useless.

The thing is, says Friedman in conversation, "She seemed to be happy. I think the whole end of Janis's life is a kind of classic set of self-destructiveness performed for reasons that are very profound and not simply understood. But it is not unheard of for bad things to happen to people just at the point when things are going good. I want to emphasize that Janis was not a suicide in the conscious sense. But as a parallel, it has been observed that suicides are often *not* depressed, rather to the contrary.

"Here Janis was making a great album. She'd met a guy who she thought was going to answer some questions for her. Everything was looking good. And it's exactly at that moment that she started heroin again. In light of which, it's hard not to look for some profound self-destructive urge underlying all of her behavior."

On Saturday afternoon, October 3, 1970, Janis Joplin bought some heroin from a dealer who came to her room at the Landmark. She used some of it and then that night went to the studio to check on the progress of the latest instrumental track. Afterward, she had two drinks with Ken Pearson at a hip local L.A. hangout and around half past midnight split up with him back at the hotel and went to her room. About an hour later, she went to the hotel lobby for cigarettes. She returned to her room and pitched forward onto her nose, which broke. The great Janis Joplin was stone-cold dead.

As reconstructed by the L.A. "coroner to the stars" Thomas Noguchi, the explanation of her final moments goes like this: Sometime after the drinks and before the cigarettes, Janis Joplin had sampled another bag of that dope, which was coursing her veins in a countdown to ultimate ecstasy as she made her way out to the lobby and back. Remnants of the last blast were found in a waste basket by her bed.

"She was more complicated, more fragile, more vulnerable underneath all that stuff," says Myra. "It's true that she was often very difficult and very coarse. She was flamboyant, she was wild, all of that stuff, but she was at the same time a complex person with a very strong puritanical streak.

"The critic Lillian Roxon wrote an article about her after Janis died. Lillian said, 'Wasn't this awful,' because she could picture Janis 10 years down the pike with this tweed suit and her hair up and so on—even at that time Lillian could see that as a possibility. If she had just not OD'd.

"I think she had as much of a chance to make it as some of her friends. She had this one close friend who was practically a street junkie and who has just gotten a degree in archeology. You couldn't get her near a drug of any kind, not even a joint. She doesn't want any part of it, and this has been for more than ten years now. People that get into the kind of trouble have to make a decision; there are no halfway measures. Janis used to say that there was no such thing as a weekend junkie. And she would have had to learn that there's no such thing as a weekend drunk either.

"Someone once said that when "Keep on Rockin'" turns into 'Nearer My God to Thee,' there are certain decisions you have to make. If Janis had lived, she might have come to that decision."

Her road manager discovered the body the next day. Everybody was shocked. And then they tugged and pulled to remove the heavy nails and take her little body off the cross.

11

GRAM PARSONS

The Lord's Burning Rain

And I saw my devil,
And I saw my deep blue sea...
—Gram Parsons, "Return of
the Grievous Angel," 1973

He was rich. He was beautiful. And, oh my, was he talented. But Gram Parsons had this problem. Not just his drug problem. Not just his drinking problem. Not just his motorcycle problem. And not just the weight problem that his drinking problem contributed to and that caused one old friend to flee from a latter-day encounter in horror. ("I couldn't wait to get out of there," she later said by way of tribute.) The problem that *really* killed him was that Gram Parsons, reprobate, was an exceedingly moral man. But then what did you expect?

He was born in the Bible Belt, somewhere to the right of the buckle, in Winter Haven, in central Florida, on November 5, 1946. He grew up a few hundred miles to the north, in Waycross, Georgia—but no matter; they know about the devil at least as

well in Waycross as in Winter Haven. His mother was a devout Christian woman. His father was an obscure country singer and songwriter named Conner who billed himself as Coon Dog, got drunk a lot, and sometimes landed in jail. In Gram's childhood home the radio was almost always on, and when it wasn't tuned to the country station and its songs of sin, it was tuned to the antidote, the gospel station with its songs of redemption. He was as steeped in ambivalence and guilt as any good Christian son of the South, torn between the preaching of his mama and the backsliding of his dad—torn perhaps like Elvis, who, after his own daddy, was Gram's biggest musical idol. But I don't need to tell you that. All you have to do is see the pictures: Gram Parsons may have naturally resembled Ricky Nelson, but the curl of that lip was willfully copied, verbatim, from the King.

The young Gram was torn again by his mama and daddy, when Mama Avis and her Coon Dog split. As one intimate of Gram's put it, Mama had decided she preferred "southern money to southern music." Southern money was exactly what Mr. Robert Parsons had, piles of it. And it's what Gram had, too, after the gentleman from Georgia adopted the boy and gave him his good name. Indeed, in those days in the late sixties and early seventies, when he was flitting from band to band, traveling around the world, getting high, getting laid, fathering an illegitimate child, and sometimes doing nothing—except of course changing the face of modern music—Gram was collecting a cool 30 grand a year from his Parsons trust fund. Which in those days was a lot of money. Not that it was enough for Gram. "When he runs out of money," said a friend, suggesting that he did run out *often*, "he gambles—and wins." Gram Parsons, you see, aspired to be the complete backslider: drinker, drugger, womanizer, and gambler.

Gram started playing and writing music in the early sixties as part of a Kingston Trio-style group called the Shilos (a poor-quality recording of which was released after Gram's death). The Shilos were popular enough at fraternity and country-club affairs, but Gram found both the group and the town stifling. Waycross, he once told a reporter, was "the kind of place that once you learn to walk, you start walkin' out of town." In 1964, Gram walked all the way up to Harvard University. Having eschewed the standard entrance test, he had been admitted solely on the strength of his essay. "What department?" a *Rolling Stone* writer would later embarrass Gram by asking. "Theology," replied Parsons. "I was into God then." Which is perhaps not so odd a way to go to the devil.

Cambridge, Massachusetts, may not be some people's idea of sin city, but for this country boy, turned on to music and then to those crazy experiments of Harvard professor Timothy Leary that he'd read about in *Life*, Cambridge was close enough. The city captivated Gram, and his first theology class at Harvard was barely over before he had decided to dispense with college entirely. Gram Parsons ate LSD and played music in the clubs and coffeehouses of Cambridge and Boston and, in four or five months, had already made his first major musical move, assembling the legendary International Submarine Band.

In 1965, a good three or four years before the phrase was coined, Gram Parsons's International Submarine Band invented country-rock, grafting rock-style lyrics and attitudes onto a base of country licks and instrumentation. By way of explaining his creation, Gram would later say: "I just passed my identification crisis and came back to country music." He was nineteen years old.

Gram became so absorbed in his music that for a time he even gave up tripping. One friend at the time went so far as to describe him as "idealistic." Gram was dedicated to making a success of the ISB. The band traveled to New York, where they failed to set the town afire, and then to Los Angeles, where Gram's ideals were stretched to the breaking point by his inability to make headway. Suddenly, Nashville producer Lee Hazelwood appeared on the scene. He liked what he heard and signed the group to his own LMI label. The resulting album was called *Safe at Home*, and if it didn't set any sales records, it made a big hit with certain segments of L.A.'s rock community. Nevertheless, financially strapped—except, presumably, for Gram—the band members went their separate way in 1967.

Gram decided to stick around L.A., trying out at open-mike

nights at country joints all over the city, then venturing further to hardcore redneck dives in the City of Industry. "I started going out there every weekend," he told an interviewer. "The first couple of times I nearly got killed; there I was in my satin bell bottoms and the people couldn't believe it. I got up on stage and sang, and when I got off a guy said to me, 'I want you to meet my five brothers. We were gonna kick your ass but you can sing real good so we'll buy you a drink instead.' Thank God I'd got on that stage. . . . " But Gram's obvious talents and his rep from the ISB record meant he wouldn't be playing open mikes for long. Soon enough, Roger McGuinn invited Parsons to join the Byrds.

Head Byrd McGuinn was so impressed with Gram and his music that he basically allowed the newcomer to remake the band. The Byrds' next two albums, *The Notorious Byrd Brothers* and the masterful *Sweetheart of the Rodeo,* released in 1968, brought country-rock to the masses—or at least to a sizable cult of them—and further burnished the growing legend of the Harvard boy from Waycross. Typically, in his rush toward destiny, Gram did not remain with the Byrds for long. After a July 1968 tour of England that culminated in an appearance at London's famed Royal Albert Hall, the band was offered a lucrative series of dates in South Africa. No longer the million-selling chart-toppers they had been, the group took the gig. But not Gram. As a southerner who had known the Deep South's own brand of apartheid, Gram lived with the stigma of it and was repulsed by the idea of touring racist South Africa. When the band said they would go anyway, with a roadie in Gram's spot, Parsons resigned. But what did you expect? Gram Parsons was a moral man.

This time Gram stuck around London, where he formed a fateful friendship with the Rolling Stones, especially Keith Richards. Impressed with his knowledge of country music as well as his authentic country drawl, Mick Jagger is said to have written the country-tinged "Wild Horses" in Gram's honor. More significantly, Keith is rumored to have introduced him to heroin. In any case, Gram's association with the Stones put him into the stratosphere of rock stardom, even as he was beginning to plumb its depths. He was twenty-one.

When he finally returned to Los Angeles, starry-eyed and full of himself, Gram was determined to put together his own "hot country band" playing its own "classic country material." This unit would be utterly and formally authentic and at the same time natural, easy, white-hot. They would write and play traditional country music that spoke directly to the times. If that was a tall order, the band Gram assembled was taller. The band included Chris Hillman, from the Byrds, on guitar; Chris Ethridge on bass; and studio hotshot "Sneeky" Peter Kleinow on pedal steel guitar. They called themselves the Flying Burrito Brothers, and soon enough, they, too, would be rock 'n' roll legend.

Their first album was titled *The Gilded Palace of Sin*, and the first line of the opening number went, "She's a devil in disguise." The second cut was "Sin City," and in it Parsons warned: "On the thirty-first floor/A gold-plated door/Won't keep out the Lord's burning rain." Gram was singing from the heart. Throughout *Gilded Palace*, released to a somewhat baffled rock-buying public in 1969, country vied with gospel, secular with religious, rural with urban, the decadent modern world with the decent traditional one. The album was a portrait of the forces warring within Gram. On the cover, Parsons could be seen wearing one of the gaudy suits custom made by Nudie, longtime tailor to the Grand Ole Opry stars—except that a second look reveals that the fancy stitches and appliquéd doodads actually depict a dizzying array of pills and pot leaves. Gram's joke. But Gram's life, too. And on *Gilded Palace*, his art.

While gearing up for the commercially all-important follow-up to the groundbreaking *Gilded Palace*, Gram Parsons wiped out on his motorcycle on a southern California highway. It would take him nearly two years to fully piece himself together from the mysteriously unspecified injuries. Some maintain he never did recover, not so surprising when you take into account that he spent a large part of his recuperation hanging around in England and the south of France with Keith Richards, who was then passing through his most decadent phase, he later admitted. Richards was also recording the most excessive, decadent of all Stones albums, *Exile on Main Street*. It was no place to get well.

Nevertheless, some claimed that Gram came back from France

looking healthier than ever. The pictures taken in France said differently: He had put on substantial weight, and the adolescent Elvis sneer had begun to develop into an expression that one formerly adoring intimate would label "sullen" and "ugly." Gram Parsons was twenty-five.

Gram did survive the recuperation and abandoned the Burritos (though he would appear on the second album, *Burrito Deluxe*). He then returned to L.A. with the songs for his first solo album, *GP*. He claimed to have grown up. He married and said he wanted to settle down.

He dismissed the Burrito experience thus: "I wanted to take the sweetness and down-home feelings of country music and create goose bumps, make a little catharsis, but it was all too frantic. Everybody was trying too hard to prove to a lot of close-minded people that we could compete with Merle Haggard." He said he was finally going to get the thing right with *GP*.

He did. "Gram Parsons is an artist with a vision as unique and personal as those of Jagger–Richards, Ray Davies, or any of the other celebrated figures," wrote Bud Scoppa in his *Rolling Stone* review. Referring to one tune as "the saddest song I've ever heard," Scoppa quickly got to the meat of it: "[Gram's] central theme has always been that of the innocent southern boy tossed between the staunch traditions and strict moral code he was born to and the complex, ambiguous modern world." *GP* was catharsis and goose bumps all the way.

But perhaps *GP* went *too* deep, *too* far. Certainly Gram seemed to have gone too far. "His hands were ridiculous the next day when I came by with my camera to ask him some more questions and take his picture," said his friend Eve Babitz of an encounter around this time. "He actually dropped his cigarette three times before getting his first one of the day lit and pouring himself a tumbler full of Sauza [tequila]." Later that same afternoon, Parsons got angry with Babitz for an innocuous, jocular aside about "white punks on dope." *GP* had seemed to confirm that Gram's *ars* would be long. But evidence coming out of the Chateau Marmont, the storied Hollywood hotel where 10 years later John Belushi would make *his* crash landing and where

Parsons camped on and off during his on-and-off marriage, suggested that his *vita* might be even more *brevis* than most.

Two weeks before he was to record his second solo album, fire destroyed Gram's Laurel Canyon home. It pretty much finished off his marriage, too. Gram went to bunk with friends; his wife went to bunk with other friends. At first, according to a photographer present for the recording sessions, it all seemed for the better. "He had split from his old lady," she reported, "and was really getting it together, hardly drinking and not doing dope." But as the album sessions drew to a close, a change occurred. Maybe Gram the perfectionist was dissatisfied with his new work. Said the photographer, "All I knew was that something was happening, and I didn't know what." Gram Parsons then decided to take a little vacation.

Phil Kaufman was Gram's road manager and friend and, as credited on the sleeve of *GP,* his "executive nanny." Which was a joke—and also pathetically true. During the weekend of September 15–16, 1973, Gram Parsons, Phil Kaufman, Michael Martin (a roadie friend), and two San Francisco women checked into the Joshua Tree Motel, 150 miles east of Los Angeles, in the desert around the Joshua Tree National Monument. The motel, one of the more obscure show-biz retreats, is a rather plain place with a swimming pool and a nice view of the desert. "He was always anxious to go there," said his manager of Gram. "It was nothing exciting . . . but he knew every bar and saloon in the area." According to the motel manager and his wife, however, the Parsons group was quiet during their stay, mostly just relaxing around the pool—until the night of September 19.

The motel manager, Frank Barbary, was awakened late that night by pounding on the window. It was the Parsons group. They said they had left Gram and gone in search of something to eat and now they had found him unconscious. Barbary immediately called an ambulance and then raced to the Parsons cabin, where he administered mouth-to-mouth resuscitation. Evidently Frank Barbary was too late. A short time later, at Hi-Valley Memorial Hospital at Yucca Valley, the inventor of country-rock, founder of the Flying Burrito Brothers, and solo artist *extraordinaire* was pronounced dead. The coroner later said it was heart failure. G.P. was twenty-six.

But the story hardly ends there. It is really only *after* his death that Gram's story takes an unexpected turn.

Robert Parsons arrived in Los Angeles and arranged to accompany the body of his stepson back to a private funeral service and interment in New Orleans, where the Parsonses now made their home. Robert Parsons wanted to make sure that there was some propriety maintained, some dignity salvaged from the whole sad, sordid affair. Robert Parsons did not bother to consult on the matter with Phil Kaufman. But then that's what got Phil mad.

Kaufman was no stranger to the illegal or the bizarre. He had helped produce Charles Manson's infamous *LIE* album when the two were doing time at Terminal Island (Phil for drugs).

The erstwhile road manager scrounged himself up an old hearse, picked up Michael Martin, and headed down to the L.A. airport to rescue his brother Gram. Phil went right out on the tarmac, big as day, and laid some bullshit on the baggage guys about having to get away quick for a hot date—so let's skip the nasty paperwork, what say, boys? But then, thought the baggage guys, who would ever want to steal a corpse? So Kaufman and Martin loaded Gram into the hearse and drove him back out to Joshua Tree, where, atop a 20-foot-high natural quartz pyre called Cap Rock they burned him, kit and kaboodle.

"It was Gram's request," said an anonymous source, "just something he had told them not too long before he died—if I go, I want to be in Joshua Tree, and I want my ashes scattered here—that sort of thing." Nevertheless, a week later the authorities arrested Michael Martin and Phil Kaufman, an executive nanny they thought might have gone too far. Kaufman was sanguine. "I'm charged with stealing a coffin," he joked. "One of the cops called it 'Gram Theft Parsons.'" As it turned out, Kaufman was right to be cool. For their sins, Kaufman and Martin were fined modestly and given suspended jail sentences.

For *his* sins, however, as he always knew he must, Gram Parsons finally faced the Lord's burning rain.

12

DUANE ALLMAN and BERRY OAKLEY

Free Birds

*D*uane Allman and Berry Oakley are buried, side by side right where their cohort in the Allman Brothers Band, Dickey Betts, once got laid. Brother Duane said it himself:

"Gregg and Duane Allman and Dickey Betts sprinkle out little piles of coke on a table in the backstage locker room where the band is sequestered and sniff it through rolled-up $100 bills. Duane calls it 'Vitamin C,' and after his second snort, he buttonholes the fellow traveler in expansive praise of Betts's guitar playing: 'Brother Dickey's as good as there is in the *world*, my man. And he's gonna be *smokin'* tonight. Listen to him on "In Memory of Elizabeth Reed." Fuck, he wrote that fuckin' song after he fucked this chick on a fuckin' tombstone in a fuckin' cemetery in Macon. On a fuckin' *tombstone, my man!*' "

Duane Allman was the head, heart, hands, feet, and lead guitar of the Allman Brothers Band. The Allman Brothers Band was the soul of southern rock, that driving, bluesy rock 'n' roll style characterized by harmonizing lead guitars and onstage stamina rivaled elsewhere only by the Grateful Dead. The Allman Brothers were Duane; younger brother Gregg, who was the voice; co-lead guitarist Betts; drummers Butch Trucks and Jai Johanny Johanson; and Berry Oakley, who played thundering bass. Duane invented the sound that inspired the southern musical revival and gave southern rock its highest moments, particularly on the watershed double live album *The Allman Brothers Band at Fillmore East.*

He also gave young white southerners a new sense of regional pride. For years southerners had been tacitly cut off from the mainstream of the hippie movement for their perceived associations with racist southern politics. In the early seventies, as southern rock became one of rock's most popular styles and Allman-inspired southern bands like Lynyrd Skynyrd, Wet Willie, Marshall Tucker, and others took up the standard, it appeared that they had even made the South and southerners fashionable.

Like all the great rock 'n' rollers, Duane Allman was more than a musician, even though he was also one of the finest musicians of his generation. He was a cultural figure, important not only for his work, but for himself: his way of life, his dress, his speech, his attitudes. And, to a generation of white non-southern hippies, blinded to the virtues of the American South, Duane was an exotic. His funky frankness, his hard-drinking, hard-drugging, motorcycle-riding, kicked-back macho style was an appealing alternative to the fading Flower Power mode, especially for the boys. Here was a long-haired hippie style that was *unquestionably* masculine. Duane, Gregg, the band, and even their equipment men, especially a bearded bruiser named Red Dog, became heroes, lionized in the counterculture bible, *Rolling Stone:*

"Red Dog remarks that the band's success had brought some changes. 'Time was, we'd blow our last five bucks on a case of beer in Flagstaff or someplace. Now it's big business.' He makes a face, then laughs aloud: 'I still get off behind the chicks, though. Man, we get chicks ever'where we go. What really knocks me clean smooth out is to get head. Did I tell you? This weird chick was eatin' me onstage at the last Fillmore East blast. Naw, the audience couldn't see it, but all the boys could.

" 'Another time, in Rochester, I was standin' against the stage wall . . . and some chick come up and unzipped me and started gobblin' me *alive,* man. The cat in the booth . . . flashed a spotlight on us. Shit, man, I didn't know what to *do.* Three thousand people out there, see, but goddamn, it felt so *good.* I thought, Well, fuck it, and I grabbed her ears and said, 'Let it eat.' ' "

If their music was among rock's most sophisticated, the Allman Brothers Band's way of life was more back-to-basics. After the introspective, hand-wringing, psychobabbling hippie era, such simplicity had its appeal—especially since we didn't yet have to worry about being sexist. The young and the dense (natural or chemically induced) were particularly attracted, as epitomized by the stoned bellow that can be heard calling out for "Whipping Post," a Brothers song, on the *Fillmore East* album. That's why the southern rockers also became known as the southern boogie bands—*boogie* being the only word some of their more woozily ardent fans could still get out.

It's almost embarrassing to someone who was once a fan and an emulator to read over some of the Allmans' press clips from today's perspective. They weren't exactly the world's greatest role models:

"Duane and Dickey lope backstage afterwards . . . 'to do some sniff,' as Dickey terms it. . . . Dickey snorts the powder and bobs his head in pleasure. 'Sheeit, my man, I druther sniff this ol' stuff than a girl's bicycle seat.' Jo Baker, a black singer with the Elvin Bishop Group, hovers nearby, eyeing the coke. Duane fixes her with a cold stare. 'Look-a-here, sister,' he says loudly, 'I'm sorry, but I got just a little bit of this shit left, so I can't give you none.' "

They also weren't the world's greatest guys, at least not *always.* But then, what cokehead is? And what rock 'n' roller? For that matter, what hippie?

Duane said that they never wanted to be anybody's role model. They just wanted to go out there and, in the band's expression, "hit the note." One recalls how Duane yelled at *Rolling Stone* photographer Annie Leibovitz when she tried to position them for a portrait. "I'm not gonna do any of that phony posin' shit for you or nobody else," he ranted. "We're just plain ol' fuckin' southern cats, man. Not ashamed of it or proud of it, neither one. Ain't no superstars here, man." The thing is, the "plain ol' fuckin' southern cat" was for Duane Allman as much a pose as Janis Joplin's red-hot mama or Jim Morrison's Lizard King. And ol' Skydog posed and acted it to the hilt.

It would be a shame if his image obscured one's appreciation of his musicianship. Duane Allman was a fine musician who played with many of the greats on many of their great recordings. It was Wilson Pickett who, for reasons we can only guess, dubbed Duane "Skydog." It was Skydog who recommended that the Wicked Pickett expand his musical territory, and then helped him do it, by covering the Beatles' "Hey Jude," a version that has become a pop classic. Following the success of that date, Duane became the main session guitarist at the renowned Muscle Shoals studio in Alamaba, backing up such leading lights of soul as Aretha Franklin, Percy Sledge, King Curtis, and Arthur Conley. His best-known, best-remembered work, session or otherwise, came when he joined Eric Clapton to record the *Layla* album, in particular the soaring title track in which the guitarists chase each other into the stratosphere.

Of course, his work with the Allman Brothers, which included the first three albums and a bit of the fourth, was none too shabby either. He immediately established a new rock idiom with the harmony guitar lines of the debut album. The live version of "Statesboro Blues" on *Fillmore East* established Duane as the premier slide guitar player in the world. With a style that had fire and flash, but also retained a depth and moodiness that others were incapable of, he futher established himself as one of the premier guitar players, period. And as a band leader, he was obviously exactly what the Allmans needed. After him, they reaped the commercial rewards that he had helped to sow, but the band ceased to mean anything.

For all Duane Allman accomplished, and as much as he would hate to admit it, there is no doubt that the milieu in which he operated and had helped create did in fact interfere with the music. For one thing, the coke can't have helped, and doing the coke was *definitely* part of living up to the image. For another thing, the increasingly uncritical, passive response of the boogie audience, attracted in part by the macho image, didn't help. Finally, part of living up to the image was riding a big hog of a motorcycle without an inordinate regard for safety measures such as helmets and speed limits. In that sense living up to the image interfered with Duane's music for all eternity. And because he was just twenty-four when he died, one can only presume that the music would have had quite a while to play yet. Considering what he had done, the future was truly full of promise.

Nonetheless, Duane Allman took his hog out one fine fall Friday afternoon for a ride to the band's communal "Big House" to wish Linda Oakley, Berry's old lady, a happy birthday. Returning home around quarter of six in the treacherous twilight, perhaps stoned, perhaps not, Duane failed to see a truck that had moved into his lane. He swerved. The bike went out of control, flipped, and landed on top of him for a 50-foot skid. His girlfriend and Oakley' sister, who had followed Duane by car several minutes later, discovered the mortally injured guitarist and stayed with him until an ambulance arrived. Resuscitated twice in the ambulance en route, Duane finally died at Macon Medical Center after three hours of emergency surgery to repair massive internal injuries, including a ruptured coronary artery. At the funeral services in Macon, the Allman Brothers Band played the blues for Duane Allman—born November 20, 1946, Nashville; raised in Daytona Beach; died October 29, 1971, Macon, Georgia.

A year and 3 days later, Berry Oakley rode away from the Big House on *his* hog and, three blocks from where Duane had crashed, ran into the back of a city bus. Berry, however, walked away from his wreck, refused medical attention, and was driven home. Two hours later, complaining of a headache, he collapsed. Four hours later, the Allman Brothers' unsinkable bassist, Berry Oakley, twenty-three, died in Macon Medical Center following emergency surgery for a massive brain hemorrhage.

Duane and Berry both died in motorcycle crashes.

But their cause of death might just as well have been white-line fever.

13

RONNIE VAN ZANT and LYNYRD SKYNYRD

More Free Birds

*L*ynyrd Skynyrd's first hit was "Freebird," a tribute to the late Duane Allman. Lynyrd Skynyrd resembled the Allman Brothers in several ways. They were a hard-driving, bluesy rock band with three harmonizing guitars, to the Allman Brothers' two. They were also a hard-drinking, hell-raising, macho-man band with a hard-drinking, hell-raising, macho-man following. In addition, Lynyrd Skynyrd was very proud to be from the South, and their shows were punctuated by rebel yells and the waving of the Stars and Bars.

Finally, with the disintegration of the Allman Brothers Band, Lynyrd Skynyrd became the standard-bearers of southern rock, its most popular proponents and its most proficient.

But in one important way, they seemed different from the Allmans. Lynyrd Skynyrd was in control of their image, not vice versa. But then, true to form, they were cut down in their prime anyway. In their wake, the myth of the southern rocker—the contemporary era's Johnny Reb—shone more brightly than ever.

The band first got together in 1966, under a variety of names, in Jacksonville, Florida, during their senior year in high school. The lineup was Gary Rossington and Allen Collins on guitar; Billy Powell on keyboards; Leon Wilkeson on bass; Bob Burns on drums; and a smallish, dirty-blond, seventeen-year-old punk named Ronnie Van Zant out front singing lead. They eventually took the name of a high school phys ed teacher, Leonard Skinner, known for his antipathy toward boys with long hair, and set off on the southern bar circuit.

It wasn't until 1972 that they were discovered at an Atlanta club called Funocchio's by Al Kooper, late of the Blues Project; Blood, Sweat & Tears; and various Super Sessions, who was looking for groups for MCA's new Sounds of the South label. A year later they recorded and released their first album, *Pronounced Leh-Nerd Skin-Nerd.*

It was produced by Kooper, who had also convinced the band to add a third guitarist, Ed King, formerly of the bubble-gum psychedelic group Strawberry Alarm Clock. When "Freebird" hit, the band was given the chance to open for the Who's *Quadrophenia* tour. They then demonstrated what seven years of playing three sets a night can do for a band. They were tight, they were relentless, and they won converts at every show.

The next album, *Second Helping,* in 1974, featured a song that was an angry and complex response to the accusations of the Neil Young song "Alabama." "In Birmingham they love the gov-'ner," sang Van Zant, referring to Alabama governor George Wallace, who had done so much to hurt the self-image of compassionate southerners throughout the sixties. "Now we all do what we can do," Van Zant continued singing, over biting guitar arpeggios. He was accepting responsibility to try for change, yet refusing to accept the guilt of failure that Young wanted to put on him. "Sweet Home Alabama," as the song was titled, after its rousing chorus, became Lynyrd Skynyrd's biggest hit, gaining them the approving attention of critics as well. Together with the word of mouth on their live shows, it finally put the band over the top. Almost quietly, *Second Helping* ascended to the number-12 slot on the pop charts and sold more than a million copies.

If they looked at first like a southern bar band jumping on the Allman Brothers/southern-rock bandwagon, Lynyrd Skynyrd quickly proved otherwise. With each album, they reached and grew. Their growth was all the more remarkable because their core audience, the boogie monsters, demanded so little, demanded in fact that they *not* change. Lacking the virtuosity of the Allmans, while at the same time forced forever to live in the shadow of that virtuosity, Lynyrd Skynyrd had to add some extra-hard work to its hard-living southern-rock formula. In fact, one gets the impression of a group of journeymen musicians who through true team effort and hard work managed to transcend themselves, achieving undeniable nobility and even a glimmer of greatness.

The only time I met Skynyrd leader Ronnie Van Zant, for an interview in his publicist's office, he was an unprepossessing, soft-spoken southern boy who couldn't look me in the eye. His hands shook uncontrollably—from nervousness as well as (of course) hangover—and he displayed a singular lack of charisma. I felt sorry for him. A few years later, he was practically the president (by acclamation) of a new youthful Confederacy and a truly inspiring figure: tough, tender, utterly self-assured, and burning with a vision for his music and his people. Even his physical presence had been augmented. He was actually larger—partly, it must be said, from the weight put on by his drinking, but larger all the same.

For all his wild ways, especially the drinking, there was none of the doomed aura that enveloped other rock 'n' roll wild men like Brian Jones and Jim Morrison. There was also none of the cokehead celebrity nastiness that sometimes emanated from his hero, Duane. Van Zant's transformation was exhilarating to witness, doubly so because too many of our rock stars seem only to degenerate with stardom.

Over the years, while the core of the band remained, some players left and others were added: Steven Gaines replaced Ed King on third guitar; Artimus Pyle replaced Bob Burns on drums; and a backup vocals trio, including Gaines's sister Cassie, was added. Lynyrd Skynyrd got even better. Never sacrificing the drive that made southern rock so physically satisfying, in 1977 they went into the studio and recorded their most thoughtful, darkest, and most compelling album. Titled *Street Survivors,* its cover shows the members of the band standing tall as they are engulfed by flames. Its most important song is a hard, bleak, cautionary tale, a Van Zant composition, supposedly directed at a drug addict friend, called "That Smell." "The smell of death surrounds you," Van Zant spat out angrily in the chorus. It was a warning to all of us, and one that Van Zant, a street survivor indeed, had clearly taken to heart. Three days after the record's release, however, on October 20, street survivor Ronnie Van Zant was dead.

Lynyrd Skynyrd left Greenville, South Carolina, the afternoon of the twentieth in a small, chartered twin-engine aircraft. They were in high spirits en route to a gig in Baton Rouge, some 600 miles away. They never made it. The plane crashed in a wooded area near Gillsburg, Mississippi, somewhat more than halfway. It had, supposedly, run out of gas.

Allen Collins survived and, despite severe injuries, crawled several miles in the dark to find help. When searchers found their way back to the wreckage, however, they discovered the bodies of Steven Gaines, his sister Cassie, and Ronnie Van Zant. They had all apparently died on impact. Rossington, Pyle, Billy Powell, Leon Wilkeson, and Collins, survived, despite serious injuries.

But Lynyrd Skynyrd did not. Not without Van Zant. It was a truly ironic end for Ronnie, a man who, almost alone among the latter-day dead rockers, had learned the lessons of the sixties. He had learned not to confuse image and reality, and he had made the choice—and was making the effort—to go on living.

14
SID VICIOUS
No Future

*A*fter the breakup of the Sex Pistols in 1978, manager Malcom McLaren propped John Simon Ritchie up in front of a motion-picture camera and had him sing Frank Sinatra's theme song, "My Way." Ritchie probably thought he was making fun of Sinatra, but the shrewd McLaren surely knew that Ritchie was making fun of himself. Ritchie *had* done it his way, *all* the way. He had become the cut-up, broken-down, shell-shocked, teetering, unfunny, infantile, idiot junkie called Sid Vicious.

John Simon Ritchie was so totally doomed from the start that there's almost something heroic in his destroying himself, quickly and in a spectacular manner, rather than dragging around forever—forever down and beaten—waiting for someone else to do it. This tormented little British sociopath went down on the front pages as a moral lesson, rather than expiring, completely unconsidered and worthless, in one or another of obscurity's rat holes. He preserved his punk integrity even unto the grave. But in the end, his method of self-destruction was not heroic. He had been the *ne plus ultra* of the punk ethos, and he then pathetically participated in his own abasement. Then he killed someone and killed himself. That's not heroic stuff.

The Sex Pistols were the group that spat on their audiences and took a shit in their record company's office. Signed by Britain's EMI Records, the band was dropped after a week when the board of directors lodged a thoroughly outraged protest against them. It

seems they called the Johnny Carson of the U.K. a "bastard," "dirty old man," "dirty fucker," and "fucking rotter" on live TV.

Subsequently signed by A&M, they were again dropped, this time for the shit-in-the-in-tray prank. By then the Sex Pistols had collected close to $200,000 in nonrefundable advances from record companies before being signed by Warner Bros. for keeps.

They released one album, *Never Mind the Bollocks, Here's the Sex Pistols,* which included the classic "Anarchy in the U.K." It also included their own version of "God Save the Queen" ("She ain't no human being"), a tribute to Elizabeth's jubilee that year. Halfway through their only tour of the U.S. the band broke up— the Sex Pistols had lasted less than 18 months. For John Simon Ritchie, who had joined later, it wasn't even that long.

Ritchie was an old college friend of Pistols lead singer Johnny Rotten (born Lydon). When founding Pistol Glen Matlock left the band in March 1977, Rotten sold the group and manager McLaren on Ritchie as the new bassist—although Ritchie couldn't in fact play the bass. Rotten also gave him a new name: Sid Vicious. "He was called Vicious," Johnny later explained, "because he was such a wanker. He couldn't fight his way out of a crisp bag." But as he demonstrated during his Pistols sojourn, he could sure make a good show of it, threatening death to reporters, brandishing knives, bike chains, and assorted other accessories of mayhem. Which is exactly why he was hired.

Reconstituted as the violent, nihilistic Vicious, the essence of the new punk era, Sid nevertheless fell into all the old show-biz traps, beginning with the one where the star believes his publicity. "If anyone overestimated their own importance," wrote British punk journalists Julie Burchill and Tony Parsons, "it was Vicious, who caused resentment amongst the Pistols by spending more time trying to become a Rock Dream than learning to play his instrument. Overcompensating for the fact that he could never attract the attention focused on a lead singer with the distinctive household horror face of Rotten, Vicious sought desperately to become the media's antidarling by taking Rotten's patented trademarks to even further extremes. He slashed his body with broken bottles whereas Rotten had only stubbed cigarettes out on his arms, attacked antagonists with a rusty bike chain whereas Rotten was content to dish out verbal lashings, and injected heroin instead of snorting amphetamine.''

Vicious did succeed in getting attention, and not just from the press. When the Sex Pistols took the stage in Dallas, Sid promptly called out, "All you cowboys are faggots!" Whereupon a storm of beer cans came down upon him and the band. In San Francisco, a punk girl seeking to express her love and admiration ran down to the stage front and punched Vicious in the nose. In appreciation, he wiped the copious blood all over his bare chest. In England, Sid, along with the rest of the band, had to worry not about expressions of love, but expressions of hate, from the skinheads, who after one gig waylaid Rotten and put him in the hospital.

As it turned out, it was love, rather than hate, that got Sid after all. Which was ironic, since Sid tried so hard to embody hate. Perhaps it was not so surprising, because within the punk milieu love and hate were often indistinguishable.

The object of Sid's love was a young, fishnet-stockinged, thick-black-mascaraed, bleached-blond product of an upper-middle-class Philadelphia suburb. A punkette rebel without a cause and onetime aspiring dancer, Nancy Spungen had gone to England to get involved in the exciting punk pop scene. She wound up a groupie and a heroin addict. The other Pistols and McLaren hated her and tried to no avail to run her out of town. Some say that Nancy Spungen was the "root of all the band's evil," but they never explain precisely why. Just because it was Nancy who introduced Sid to heroin addiction (or so say some) doesn't mean that without Nancy Sid would've stayed clean. Hardly.

The two were sad, tormented children caught together in the world's biggest, stupidest chicken-dare stunt with no way out. Some say she was Sid's first-ever girlfriend; some even say that, until Spungen, Sid was homosexual. In any case, if in the midst of their drug psychosis à deux they were able to share something remotely like love, maybe they were each other's pitiful best hope and finest moment. Witness an incident recorded by Burchill and Parsons, in which Sid and Nancy do their version of the balcony scene from *Romeo and Juliet* through a punk looking glass darkly:

"As the band prepared to embark on a world tour, 'Belsen Was a Gas,' a song Sid Vicious had composed for a previous band, was introduced into their set. After being the only member of the band to turn up for a rehearsal, Vicious tried to end it all by jumping from a hotel's third-story window but was thwarted by the sheer brute strength of Nancy Spungen when she grabbed his belt and plunked him out of the cold night air.

"Sid celebrated his new lease on life by banging Nancy's head against the wall until her screams brought the police, who carted the courting couple off to the cells together with various substances for analysis."

All things being relative, it was, I suppose, love of a sort.

The world tour for which the Pistols were then preparing was their famous first and last tour of the States. In keeping with their stated antipathy toward the media and the hip, media-center cities, it took a rather perverse course, primarily through the heart of their nonsupport in the southern Bible Belt. Nevertheless, as a traveling sideshow that was getting a lot of press attention anyway, they managed to draw sellout crowds to places like Randy's Rodeo bar in Texas. By the time the tour self-aborted in San Francisco, they were the talk of the nation.

McLaren saw the pot of gold. Rotten became simply disgusted. "Malcolm was setting me up to be another Rod Stewart, and when I kicked back he didn't like it," said the lead singer, who precipitated the band's disintegration by walking out. "I won't work again with any of them, and that's no great pity." Contemptuously telling off his ex-bandmates, Rotten added, "Sid can go off and kill himself and nobody will care." He then split for London, via New York.

After a brief hiatus in New York, Rotten returned to the U.K. and put together a critically well-received new band called Public Image Limited (PIL). Sid and Nancy went straight to London.

While they were there, Nancy was threatened with deportation following a fight with some journalists and Sid performed "My Way" for his manager's camera.

Next, the couple returned to New York. Their arrival was auspicious. Sid, obviously stoned, had to be carried off the plane in New York and rushed to a nearby hospital. He was released the next day and registered with Nancy at New York's famous artists' residence, the Hotel Chelsea on Twenty-Third Street.

For the next two months, Sid and Nancy sallied forth to sample the new-wave scene that had been catalyzed by groups like the Ramones and the Sex Pistols and that, in August 1978, was still the hippest thing going. Sid and Nancy drank and took a lot of drugs and got the star treatment from their fellow punks—which could range anywhere from a request for an autograph to a fist in the face. And then sometime on the morning of October 10, Nancy Laura Spungen, twenty, was stabbed three times in the abdomen in the bathroom of the Chelsea room she shared with Sid. Fatally. Vicious, saying he had found the body, called the police. They came and picked it up. Two days later, the police came back and picked up Sid, booking him on suspicion of murder.

This finally got Sid the kind of lavish, front-page worldwide attention that John Simon Ritchie could only have dreamed of. Take that, Johnny Rotten! Five days after his arrest, Vicious was back on the scene, released on $50,000 bail. He was the hottest thing on the scene and presumably enjoying it. He found a new girlfriend and moved into her Greenwich Village apartment. His mother, who had flown over during his troubles, joined him there. And he resumed his heroin habit.

Within two months, after a bar fight with Patti Smith's younger brother, Todd, who brought charges, Sid's bail was revoked. He was remanded to New York's notorious Riker's Island prison. After what can only have been two harrowing months—not only fending for himself in the brutal inmate society of Riker's, but kicking heroin, too—Vicious was again released on bail. This time, for good.

Returning to his girlfriend's apartment, Vicious managed to

make a smack connection and within hours of exiting Rikers had tied off and poked a celebratory needleful of junk into his arm. As is so often the case with ex-junkies who fall off the wagon, the old dose proved to be too much.

His girlfriend and mother found the corpse, and that night on the "CBS Evening News," Walter Cronkite, America's favorite uncle, solemnly recited Sid's obituary in front of the entire U.S. of A. Sid Vicious had truly arrived, while the tragedy of John Simon Ritchie, twenty-one years old, had come to its inevitable, doomed end.

Almost.

There is a weird postscript to the story. Just a few months later, Sid's skinny, wasted-looking young mother was arrested in England for possession of various semihard drugs. Rumor had it that she, too, had become a junkie. Like son, it seems, like mother.

15
KEITH MOON

Happy Jack Was a Man

But they couldn't prevent
Jack
From being happy.
— *"Happy Jack," the Who,*
1966

*E*ventually the fun goes out of it. Everybody loved Keith Moon, the clown—including, of course, Moon himself. Everybody loved the way he carried on, mugging through shows, cutting up in the studio, cavorting through his private life, and, perhaps most famously, destroying hotels around the world. But eventually, where there is no restraint and no direction, the fun of a clown like Keith Moon starts to leach away, and soon enough the clown has become something else.

During the Who's 1976 tour of the States, 10 years after they had recorded "Happy Jack," their first hit single, in a room in the Navarro Hotel in New York City—the *last* hotel in New York City that would have him—it happened for the man they liked to call "Moon the Loon." What should have been the world's funniest rock star making his customary road mischief wound up looking like Martin Sheen in his Saigon Hotel room at the beginning of *Apocalypse Now*. And it *was* an apocalypse for Keith.

Who manager Bill Curbishley and his wife, Jackie, were asleep in their room at the Navarro when the phone rang. A voice the manager recognized as Moon's stated simply: "I'm going to throw all the furniture out the window."

Curbishley had been here before. Too tired to fight Moon this time or to humor him, he said irritatedly, "Well, throw it out the window, then," and hung up. But something about the call disturbed Jackie Curbishley, and finally she prevailed upon her husband to go check. Curbishley went upstairs to the door of Moon's room, which was slightly ajar.

The manager recounted the ensuing minutes. "I tried to open it and I couldn't; there was something in the way. I managed eventually to get it open and went into the bedroom and there was Moon. The whole of the apartment was fucking saturated with blood.

"He was lying on the floor. . . . He had kicked a painting and the glass had broken and he had cut his foot right in the instep, in the vein. With every heartbeat it was spurting out black blood. He'd lost fucking pints.

"I got a towel and put a tourniquet on his leg, then phoned . . . our security guy. I told him to get a cab to take us to the nearest hospital. I picked Moon up and put him over my shoulder . . . and the blood was pissing over me.

"I got him in the elevator, got him downstairs, and the bottom of the elevator was covered in blood.

"That was one time he definitely would have died, because there was no one there, he had lost so much blood, he was too weak even to get to a phone. There had been other times when he had been near death. But that was Moon."

Yes, that was Moon—and then, all of a sudden, one day it wasn't.

Keith was born in Wembley, England, on August 23, 1947, the first child of auto mechanic Alfred and housemaid Kitty

Moon. A class clown with mediocre grades, he played trumpet in a scout group. But, says his mother, "as soon as Keith came in contact with the drums, that was all he seemed keen on." At fifteen he dropped out of school and began playing in local bands, supplementing his income with a dizzying succession of day jobs.

In 1964, while playing with the Beachcombers, an anomalous English surf-music group (surely a clue to the secret of Moon's unique drumming style), Keith auditioned for a band called the Detours. A mutual friend introduced drummer and band at the Detours' regular Thursday-night pub gig, asking if the boy—Moon was only seventeen—could sit in. Detours bassist John Entwistle described what happened next: "Dyed ginger hair, a brown shirt, brown tie, brown suit, brown shoes. He looked just like a little gingerbread man. He got up on the kit, and we said, 'Can you play "Road Runner"?' . . . And he played it, and we thought, Oh this is the fellow. He played it perfectly." He also, as Entwistle recalled, "broke the session drummer's bass-drum pedal that he'd had for twenty years and mucked up the hi-hat," another clue to the secret of Moon's drum style and a preview of wreckage to come.

The Detours, of course, soon became the Who, and though Pete Townshend would write the songs and gain the lion's share of the glory, Moon would be their soul and inspiration. "When Keith joined," Entwistle went on to say, "we started developing what was really the Who style."

In 1965, the Who recorded their first single, "I Can't Explain." "Moon was incredible," said the session's ordinarily more reserved producer. "He could do things with drums that probably haven't been done since. He was a great drummer. Complete nutcase, but a great drummer." "I Can't Explain" made a very strong chart showing in England, though not in America. Their third single, "Substitute," became the band's first British number one. And that great drummer, now nineteen, had already made his name, both musically and otherwise, stepping to the forefront as no rock 'n' roll drummer ever had.

But there were heavier overtones in his giddy notoriety.

Describing the recording of "Substitute," Who biographer Dave Marsh writes: "Moon did his usual wild man act, although he was later to deny any memory of doing the session and in fact panicked when he first heard 'Substitute' on the radio, certain that the Who was finally eliminating him and had already begun recording with someone else. . . . As Townshend later pointed out, this memory lapse is a pretty good indication of how far gone on pills and booze Moon was even in those early days. [He was already] acquiring a reputation in the press as *the* rock 'n' roll delinquent." But they hadn't seen nothing yet.

Nineteen sixty-seven was the year of the Who's American breakthrough. After seizing the attention of the music business and media from their bottom-of-the-bill slot on a Murray the K package show, they went on to headline at the Fillmore West. Most important, they appeared on closing night of the Monterey Pop Festival. While some feel that Hendrix stole that show and some, Janis, and some, Otis, Dave Marsh records his impression thus: "When the festival ended, four names remained [all of them, I might add, no longer remaining]: Otis Redding, Jimi Hendrix, Janis Joplin, and the Who." The Who also broke through to AM radio with their first Top 10 American single, "I Can See for Miles." *Rolling Stone* voted them best rock 'n' roll band of the year. Keith Moon, who perhaps took the idea of *break*through too literally, destroyed his first hotel.

The first recorded instance of Moon's hotel destruction came during a tour that summer with the Blues Magoos and Herman's Hermits. Keith used some cherry bombs he'd purchased at a roadside stand in Georgia to blow up a toilet. But it wasn't until the tour got to Flint, Michigan, that the fun—and the Moon legend—really started. Keith claimed afterward that the occasion had been his twenty-first birthday. In reality, he had only *said* that so they wouldn't bar him from legally drinking in the state.

Anyway, it was always one of his own favorite Keith Moon stories, and he recalled it often and fondly: "That's how I lost my front tooth. . . . We were all around the Holiday Inn pool (in Flint, Michigan), Herman's Hermits and myself. I was twenty-one and they started giving me presents. . . . I'd started drinking about ten o'clock in the morning and I can't remember the show. Then the record company had booked a big room in the hotel . . . for a party.

"As the hours went on it got louder and louder, and everybody started getting well out of their minds. . . . The Premier Drum Company had given us a huge birthday cake. . . . I picked up the cake, all five tiers, and hurled it in the throng. People'd started picking up the pieces and hurling it about. Everybody was covered in marzipan and icing sugar and fruit cake. . . .

"By the time the sheriff came in I was standing there in my underpants. I ran out, jumped in the first car I come to, which was a brand-new Lincoln Continental. It was parked on a slight hill, and when I took the handbrake off, it started to roll and it smashed straight through the [fence surrounding the] pool and the whole Lincoln Continental went into the Holiday Inn swimming pool with me in it.

"Today I can think of less outrageous ways of going than drowning in a Lincoln Continental in a Holiday Inn swimming pool, but at the time I had no thoughts of death whatsoever. . . . "

Remembering a physics lesson about equalizing pressure, Moon managed to save himself this time. "So I went back to the party, streaming water, still in me underpants. The first person I see is the sheriff and he's got his hand on his gun. . . . I started to leg it out the door and I slipped on a piece of marzipan and fell flat on my face and knocked out my teeth."

The bill, which also included a charge for repainting six cars at which someone in the Moon party had aimed a chemical fire extinguisher, came to $24,000. "I wasn't even making half that on the tour," said Moon. So they took up a collection and among the three bands and assorted functionaries managed to pay. Nevertheless, the Who were henceforth forever barred from the Holiday Inn chain, and Keith Moon's reputation was thereby stretched around the globe.

Over the next 11 years, Moon continued to hone that reputation relentlessly. "I get bored, you see," he told another English reporter. "There was a time in Saskatoon, in Canada . . . I took out me hatchet and chopped the hotel room to bits. The televi-

sion. The chairs. The dresser. The cupboard doors. The bed."
Which sounds almost reasonable, as Dave Marsh points out, until
you think about it. . . . For one thing, what other rock 'n' roll
drummer ever packed a hatchet?

The continual destruction became a bit expensive, even for the
Who, according to Moon. "We were smashing up probably ten
times if not more than we were earning," he said in the mid-
seventies. But then Moon never did pay much attention to the
money. Later, cautioned by his accountant that as a millionaire he
must begin spending more or wind up paying the tax man, Moon
gleefully swung into action. "Six weeks later I'd spent it all. I'd
bought four houses, a hotel, eight cars, a swimming pool, tennis
courts, expensive wristwatches—that fell apart—a riverside bungalow furnished in French Renaissance period furniture. I'd
spent it all." Then Moon laughed heartily.

The first time Moon's antics stopped being funny—for Moon
himself as much as for his public—came on January 4, 1970.
Following the success of *Tommy* in 1969, the Who were certified
rock superstars, up there with the Stones, and Keith Moon, much
to his satisfaction, was a sought-after, fawned-over international
celebrity. On the night of January 4, accompanied by his wife
and Larry "Legs" Smith of the Bonzo Dog Band and Smith's
girlfriend, Moon was headed north in his chauffered Rolls-Royce
for the star-studded opening of a discotheque in Hertsfordshire.
When they arrived, the car was set upon by angry skinheads, and
chauffeur Neil Boland, who also functioned as Keith's body-
guard, got out to calm them. Mayhem ensued. A drunken Moon
got behind the wheel. Boland fell. Moon evidently hit the
accelerator, and the wheels of the Rolls-Royce crushed the
chauffeur's head. He was DOA at the hospital. Though Moon did
admit to the drinking, the coroner ruled Boland's death accidental. "Nevertheless, Keith sank into an alcoholic depression for
the next three months. He was shaken out of it only when the
Who went back on the road in America, back to the fantasy world
in which Keith Moon was needed."

By 1973, Moon's marriage, among other things, was collaps-
ing. Several destructive factors were at work. Moon was utterly

and irrevocably alcoholic; he was brutally flagrant about his infidelity; and his laughter had revealed a flip side in his fiery temper, generally aimed at wife, Kim, sometimes wounding daughter, Mandy, in the process. Keith's personal roadie, Dougal Butler, describes one night at dinner chez Moon, as recounted below.

First, of course, the host himself was hopelessly late. Upon his arrival, rather than sitting down peacefully to eat, he laced into his wife concerning the location of a valued caftan. Before long, Moon lobbed a milk bottle at Kim. A ricochet of broken glass cut [daughter] Mandy on the face. When Butler tried to calm his boss, Moon promptly delivered him a roundhouse right, whereupon the two fell to the floor in combat as Kim and Mandy dissolved in tears. Shortly thereafter, Kim, with Mandy in tow, decamped permanently.

Moon was regretful, but finally he was resigned, observing with chilling honesty: "My way of life is not conducive to any kind of stable family relationship. I am not close to my daughter, Mandy. I think she's nine, but I forget."

As his home life disintegrated, Moon's looniness got even loonier—more compulsive, more dangerous, more desperate. Dougal Butler describes a day on the road from 1975, trying to get Keith from L.A. to a gig in San Francisco three hours hence.

"Moonie's room is in pitch-black, which is not surprising as he blows out all the lights in the chandelier the night before by hurling the 30-inch Hitachi . . . color TV set at them. All over the floor, there's glass, bedclothes, broken bottles, tipped-up ashtrays and . . . right in the middle of it is Moonie, stretched out on his back, completely out of it and stark bollock naked. . . . " Butler eventually woke him, whereupon Moon demanded brandy. When Butler denied him brandy, he ordered a few of his "pick-me-ups"—a plastic-boxed assortment of ups and downs—which Dougal eventually located in the muck. Moon gobbled a fistful and began to get himself together. Butler continues.

"But Moonie's idea of getting himself together for a trip is not everyone's idea of same. He is not overly concerned about his toothbrush or . . . pyjamas. . . . No. He is more worried about his buffalo horns which he buys a few days back at Nudie's, the western shop. . . .

"At last we find them, stuffed down behind a sofa, and Moonie fits them to his head."

By the time they got to San Francisco, Moon was incoherent and gelatinous and had to depart the plane in a wheelchair. Finally Dougal helped him to a semisubhuman condition and got him onstage.

Butler goes on. "But, suddenly, Moonie doesn't know what he's meant to be playing. . . . Pete Townshend spins round and screams at Moonie: 'Play faster, you cunt. Faster!'

"So Moonie plays another thirty seconds at a passable clip. Then his head starts to go. His feet stop. He drops one of his sticks and I can see that he is about to do a diver into the biggest of his floor-standing Premier tom-toms. . . . "

Dougal Butler called San Francisco's Free Doctor Service, hoping for a hip MD who wouldn't turn them all in. Within a minute, the hippie doc arrived, looking like the underground comics' "Fabulous Furry Freak Brothers." He handed Dougal one of two giant hypos.

As Butler tells it, "The good doc tells me that what we have to do is inject both ankles at the same time. . . . So we lurk under the drum riser, syringes at the ready, until the doc mouths, 'One, two, three . . . GO!' and boff! It's into both ankles right on the button.

"Well, Moonie makes like some old bag who's being goosed for the first time in thirty years! Pretty soon he's drumming up such a storm that Townshend turns around and screams at him: *'Play slower, you cunt, slower!'* "

And thus did Dougal Butler save the day. As comic as the scene may sound, at the same time it's not funny at all.

By 1973, the drugs and alcohol and general excess were at last, as they always will, beginning to win out. It showed in the fuck-ups in his personal life. Even more important to Keith, who considered the band his only *true* family, it showed in the music. Says Dave Marsh of Moon's performance that year on *Quadrophenia:* "Keith stumbled through the sessions, but for the first time, he played without the fire and inspiration that had always been the driving force of the Who. His playing was competent but . . . nothing more." There was, however, one small epiphany, according to Marsh.

"The conclusion of the album, and one of the last things recorded, was 'Love Reign O'er Me.' Jimmy, the mod hero . . . has reached the end of his rope and is moodily sitting on a rock at sea, with the waves crashing in front of him and his thoughts and emotions equally turbulent. To evoke the atmosphere, [co-producer Ron] Nevison and Townshend set Moon up with a full complement of the studio's percussion accessories and let him bang away. At the end, he simply arose and dumped the tubular bells into the rest, looking on joyfully as everything collapsed in a thunderous heap. It was the closest he'd come to a hotel room in his entire studio career, and it was his last great moment on record."

At the age of twenty-six, the greatest drummer in rock was washed up. Two years later, he was doing his blood-splattered *Apocalypse Now* psycho number alone in a room at the Navarro Hotel. By 1978, everybody began to acknowledge that, if the band couldn't go on without him, they also couldn't continue any longer *with* him. They carried him through one more album, *Who Are You*. But concerned as they were, they didn't believe that it would actually be his last.

"Moonie played games," the album's producer, Glyn Johns, said. "You never knew if he was drunk or not drunk, why he was pretending to be drunk or why he was drunk, if he was. . . . It could have been insecurity, it could have been anything.

"Peter was really worried about the fact that he was drinking as much as he was. We all were. Pete was instrumental in trying to get Moonie to stop drinking. I remember he did for a while. But there was always the overriding thing, it seemed, that everybody believed he was totally indestructible, because he abused himself far more than any other human being I ever met."

Keith Moon had taken on all the familiar signs of the advanced alcoholic: He was fat and bloated, and his cheeks carried a new ruddiness that mocked his healthful apple cheeks of old. He was thirty but he looked forty-five. He could no longer do his job: On one of the latest album's songs, "Music Must Change," he fucked up so continuously and badly that Townshend left the drums off the final mix entirely. All that stood between him and losing his job was Pete Townshend's sentimentality. The others were ready to give him the old heave-ho. Meanwhile, Moon went on and off the wagon and felt convinced he was getting better.

"I feel I've got a sense of purpose," says Keith. "In the two years [the Who took] off, I was really drifting away with no direction, no nothing. I'd try to do things and get involved in projects, but nothing ever came close to the feeling I get when I'm working with the guys. Because it's fun, but at the same time I know I've gotta discipline myself again."

It is probably a pathetic indication of both the strength of his resolve to be disciplined and its weakness that he died of an overdose of Heminevrin, a muscle relaxant used to help cure alcoholism and the side effects of withdrawal.

On September 6, 1978, Keith attended a midnight screening of the new movie *The Buddy Holly Story* and afterward a Buddy Holly birthday party (Holly was born on September 7) hosted by Paul McCartney.

Moon and his girlfriend, Annette Walter-Lax, returned, at around quarter of five in the morning, to their apartment, where Keith took a handful of his Heminevrin and went to sleep. Around seven-thirty, he awoke hungry and made himself a steak-and-champagne breakfast, downed another handful of Heminevrin, and went back to bed. At four-thirty, Walter-Lax found she could not rouse him and called a doctor, who called an ambulance. But Keith Moon was beyond the ministrations of ambulance paramedics, beyond even the magic of hippie doctors and their ankle shots.

Keith Moon was beyond the limits of his own indestructibility. He had just turned thirty-one. The fun was over.

16
JOHN BELUSHI
Blue Brother

*Y*ou can see why Belushi's wife was angry at Bob Woodward for his book *Wired*. Talk about not too fucking funny anymore—John Belushi might even have Keith Moon beat. By Woodward's account, the guy turned into a thoroughly shameless shit heel, not to mention a bottomless drug hole, in the last years of his life—a life that had only 33 years in total. He became an unfunny, unesthetic, raving Hollywood creep, bossing around friends as well as employees, indulging his every whim, lying, cheating, and on at least one occasion even *stealing* (cocaine, of course, from a friend and sometime connection).

Yes, there were reasons for all this, some of them deep in John Belushi's fat body, funny-looking face, and second-generation-immigrant psyche. But John Belushi was no Janis Joplin, no hopeless ugly-duckling high school reject. Where Janis was constantly spurned by high school classmates for her acned ugliness and overcompensating obnoxious behavior, John was made captain of the football team. Where Janis was voted Ugliest Man on Campus, John was voted homecoming king. Yes, there were mitigating factors in John Belushi's decline, but they were no excuse. You pity Janis (perhaps feeling superior). You want to hit Belushi, to slap him and spank him and tell him to fuck off. You want to hurt him, because he knew better. Just as Hendrix knew better, but much more so. (Hendrix's death was *truly*

accidental, a result of living dangerously, not suicidally.)

Half of Belushi's act was making fun of the kind of arrogant, out-of-it show-biz cretin that he eventually became. Maybe he got swept up in the adulation, which compensated for his absent father and lower-middle-class-in-the-midst-of-an-upper-middle-class-neighborhood upbringing and his funny face. Maybe, on the other hand, with him being football captain and homecoming king in high school and *always* coming out on top, John Belushi just got hopelessly spoiled. Maybe, but it's no excuse.

John Belushi was born on January 24, 1949, in Chicago, where his father, Adam, an Albanian immigrant, worked in a restaurant. Eventually, Adam scrimped and saved enough to open two of his own restaurants in Chicago and to move his family to the Chicago suburb of Wheaton (also the hometown, as it turns out, of Watergate reporter and Belushi biographer Bob Woodward). Both Belushi restaurants were called the Olympia and would later lend their name to a third establishment, the greasy spoon of the "chizburger" skits on "Saturday Night Live." Though Belushi's father was almost always working—and so almost always away from home, frequently sleeping at one or the other of the Chicago joints—his restaurants finally went broke, forcing him to become a bartender.

Though being the son of an immigrant Albanian bartender was apparently a painful thing for John in affluent Wheaton, he was never shunned for it. He gained some of his high school's highest honors, grid captain and homecoming king, and Most Humorous, too. Not to mention a cute girlfriend named Judy Jacklin. John acted in several high school plays and loved it, impressing his drama teacher.

When graduation rolled around in 1967, it was clear to John that he wanted to act or play football for a living. When he aced the audition for a spot with a local summer-stock troupe, he forgot about football and chose acting. "That's what I want to do," he told his teacher afterward, according to *Wired*. By Woodward's account, the man who ran the audition called the teacher to say of young Belushi: "He's the most talented son of a bitch I've ever seen."

After knocking around a couple of colleges and putting together his own comedy troupe, Belushi auditioned for Chicago's Second City company in February 1971. Second City was the illustrious alma mater of Elaine May, Mike Nichols, David Steinberg, Alan Alda, Joan Rivers, and Alan Arkin, among many others. Once more, he was magic. At twenty-two, John became the youngest company member ever. Six months later, the *Chicago Daily News* reviewer had this to say about the Second City show: "We all have our personal favorites, however, and mine was John Belushi, who has only to step out on the stage to start me tittering like a schoolboy." For the 18 or so months he was with the troupe, his reviews only got better. His fame spread, and a young director putting together a revue in New York heard about his incredible Joe Cocker caricature. Next stop, Greenwich Village—and *Lemmings*.

Lemmings led to *The National Lampoon Radio Hour* and then another well-received revue, *The National Lampoon Show,* and regular paychecks—a very rare thing in acting—not only for himself, but for his live-in, Judy Jacklin, who joined the *Lampoon* art department. Then in 1975, via recommendations from Chevy Chase and others, *Lemmings* led Belushi to Lorne Michaels, who was putting together a late-night, youth-oriented, live show for NBC-TV, to be called "Saturday Night." Already enough of a prima donna that he became angry when asked to audition (Radner and Aykroyd didn't have to), John finally did his Samurai pool hustler, brought the house down, and got the part.

According to Woodward, there was a lot of cocaine backstage at *Lemmings,* and Belushi was heavily into it, heavily enough that one NBC exec was said to be "terrified" when he heard that Michaels had hired Belushi, due to Belushi's drug rep. Coke was also all over the place at "Saturday Night," and by the end of the first year Belushi was already starting to pay less attention to the show and more to drugs. He was dropping up to 500 bucks a week on his precious nose candy. His self-destructive behavior ballooned along with his salary, his celebrity, and his weight.

"One day John would say, 'I'm getting away from drugs,' and

the next, 'I can handle drugs,'" writes Woodward. "Judy didn't believe either statement. She knew coke made John less sensitive, and apparently he had to be that way to perform. He feared, sometimes," Woodward adds on a familiarly pathetic, but evidently verifiable, note, "that people only laughed at him because he looked funny."

Still several years away from being *truly* rich and famous, by fall of 1976, John, at Judy's insistence, had already seen a doctor about his drug intake. The doctor, as *Wired* reports, jotted down his new patient's specs thus: "Smokes 3 packs a day; alcohol: drinks socially; medications: Valium occasionally; marijuana 4 to 5 times a week; cocaine—snort daily, main habit; mescaline—regularly; acid—10 to 20 trips; no heroin; amphetamines—four kinds; and barbiturates (Quaalude habit)."

When he insisted that John stop the coke, Belushi was indignant. "I give so much pleasure to so many people," he railed melodramatically. "Why can I not get some pleasure for myself?"

"Because," answered the doctor, "you'll kill yourself."

Michael O'Donoghue, his colleague at "Saturday Night Live," put a more romantic spin on Belushi's habit. "What you have to remember is that it's that very self-destructive drive, that crazed death-oriented gusto that puts the edge on his performance. It gives him the edge and puts him over the edge.

"You see, John has a phase he's got to work through—the star trip. He's young, probably never had much money, and now he's got limos and all this nose powder. John's got a real Judy Garland personality sometimes. He wants to grab the world and snort it."

Nevertheless, by the end of 1976, Belushi appeared to be taking his new doctor's advice—up to a point—and had reconciled with Judy. On New Year's Eve, after nine years of living together, he and Judy were married in Colorado, honeymooning in a beautiful $200-a-day mountaintop chalet.

The idyll was short-lived. Within a month, Judy was on the phone threatening one of John's coke connections with legal repercussions and again imploring John to see a psychiatrist, which he did on and off for four months in the spring. And when he finally stopped seeing the doctor entirely, it was only after "explaining to Judy that he didn't have a problem anymore." However, hard as it may have been for Judy to believe, let alone tolerate, John's "problem" was just beginning.

In 1977, John went Hollywood, playing a cameo in *Goin' South,* a cowboy flick directed by and featuring Jack Nicholson, and starring in *National Lampoon's Animal House.* Belushi arrived completely wired and hostile on the set of *Goin' South,* fingering a knife and complaining about the hotel accommodations. That evening, he shoved the film's sixty-year-old coproducer, thus precipitating a brawl with the man's outraged partner, a cool customer used to dealing with petulant stars. Only an apology from Belushi and some fancy mouthwork on the part of his manager prevented the neophyte film actor from being blacklisted in Hollywood before he'd even started.

Despite his insistence on getting stoned for many scenes, as well as on approving the film's music, Belushi was better behaved on the *Animal House* set. And when the box office figures on the film finally rolled in some 12 months later, John Belushi had earned his license to kill.

In the interim before movie stardom hit, Belushi returned to "SNL." He was sloppy and inattentive in rehearsals and obviously reading from cue cards during broadcasts. The best thing he did, probably his last good TV performance, was a short film by "SNL" writer Tom Schiller entitled *Don't Look Back in Anger,* which aired in March 1978. The film shows an elderly John reminiscing in the "Not Ready for Prime Time Cemetery" about his now-deceased colleagues. "They all thought I'd be the first to go," he says. "I was one of those 'live fast, die young, leave a good-looking corpse' types, you know." But he wasn't the first to go, he says in the punchline, " 'cause I'm a dancer!" And then he does a little jig through the graveyard. "[Lorne] Michaels thought it was prophecy," Woodward would discover. "John would outlast them all."

Animal House hit big, with John Belushi again standing out, this time in the role of king fuck-off and gross-out Bluto. On a $3-million investment, the movie returned $60 million. Belushi promptly signed to do Steven Spielberg's next movie, an epic comedy called *1941*, for $350,000 as part of a more than $2 million, three-picture deal with Universal. Then, on October 16, 1978, John Belushi appeared on the cover of *Newsweek.* The Albanian from Wheaton had now truly arrived. Not surprisingly, John Belushi wanted more.

John Belushi had played in a rock 'n' roll band for several years in high school, and he had grown up in the sixties and seventies, that golden age of rock 'n' roll. He was part of a generation that recognized its true stars not in movies or on TV but in rock 'n' roll. Though his style was ultimately the comedy equivalent of rock 'n' roll and certifiably part and parcel of the rock 'n' roll era, it still *wasn't* rock 'n' roll, and he was not a rock 'n' roll star. And thus, in his mind, he *hadn't* arrived. Not yet.

The Blues Brothers started as a joke, a crowd warm-up act at "SNL" broadcasts, but the schtick soon became probably the most important thing in John's life. After persuading Lorne Michaels to let him and Aykroyd appear on the show as the Blues Brothers, while using the success of *Animal House* as his club, Belushi managed to get Atlantic Records to fork over $125,000 for a record. On January 24, 1979, John turned thirty and the Blues Brothers LP, *Briefcase Full of Blues,* recorded live at the Universal Amphitheater in L.A., hit number one on the charts. Though critics familiar with the original sixties material dismissed the Blues Brothers as a spoiled TV star's toy, a whole new audience apparently took the Blues Brothers' R & B as the real thing. Belushi was a rock 'n' roll star. Now he had it all.

Of course, having it all still wasn't enough. Now John would have to start living the rock 'n' roll-star life, or at least his fantasy of it. Lorne Michaels described one instance. "One week, during his last season, I believe, we had built the whole show around John, who was playing then NBC boss Freddie Silverman. John had been up with Keith Richards for three days when he arrived for the dress rehearsal. He was laid out on the couch in his dressing room, burnt out and moaning and worthless. And he looked terrible, too. Eyes closed, he was moaning that he couldn't possibly go on. I was furious with him, and I called for the NBC doctor, who examined him while I was standing there and said, 'His lungs are filled with fluid. If he goes on tonight, the odds are fifty-fifty that he'll die.' Livid, I said, 'I'll *accept* those odds.'

"One of John's eyes popped open, the eyebrow raised, and he looked at me. Then he got up, changed into costume, and did a great show. The note from the doctor didn't work."

By the following fall, Belushi and partner Aykroyd had quit "SNL" and were in Chicago filming the Blues Brothers movie, directed by *Animal House* director John Landis. The film was running way over budget and way behind schedule, and everybody in Hollywood—everybody everywhere, it seemed—knew why. The director finally had had enough, and he marched over to his star's dressing-room trailer and opened the door.

Bob Woodward describes the scene in *Wired:* "There sat Belushi, a five-foot-nine ghastly, bloated, semi-adult parody of Bluto. His curly black hair was disheveled; his gaze was fixed at a point several feet in front of his eyes. Courvoisier cognac had been spilled all over. There was urine on the floor. On a table was a mound of cocaine. . . .

" 'John, you're killing yourself!' Landis shouted.

"John gave no sign, not even a shrug, that he was comprehending.

"Landis . . . scooped up the white powder, carried it over to the toilet and flushed it.

"John stood unsteadily, muttering, and began advancing on Landis—220 pounds to Landis' 165. Landis . . . reeled back and hit John square in the face. John went down.

"John didn't get up, and at first he didn't move. Then he lowered his head and burst into tears. 'I'm so ashamed, so, so ashamed.' "

His shame didn't last long, however. Within hours, he was crying to his wife that the studio was making him the scapegoat for their own ineptitude. John Belushi was completely out of control.

A few months later, at Judy's urging, John Belushi, who had once made merciless fun of the drug and drinking habits of pampered rock stars, hired a babysitter to help him control his own habits. Smokey Wendell was an ex-Secret Service agent who had previously helped pampered rock star Joe Walsh stay off drugs. On and off for the rest of Belushi's life, Smokey would accompany him everywhere, including to the bathroom, and live with John in his home or hotel suite. John would argue with Wendell and try to run away from him and pout when Wendell would discover John's latest secret cache of coke. Sometimes the two of them would have playtime together, Belushi waking Smokey up at five in the morning to play a few hands of gin rummy or to watch TV. Wendell was his paid mommy and his paid pal. It was, as John would have at one time recognized, a thoroughly revolting spectacle—almost as revolting as John on drink and drugs.

It also didn't work. Smokey would go on vacation. Or John would fire him. Or John would manage to escape him temporarily. And eventually, understandably, even the inhumanly patient Smokey would get worn out and quit. John continued drugging and drinking, at any excuse. When *1941* flopped, he went on a binge. When *The Blues Brothers* hit, he went on a binge. When he took his first romantic lead role, in *Continental Divide,* he went on a binge because he was worried he couldn't handle it. When the director said he should put more gray in his hair for a scene in *Neighbors,* he went on a binge because he disagreed.

As they say about drinkers, when he wasn't doing it to forget, he was doing it to celebrate. And when he wasn't doing it to celebrate, he was just doing it, compulsively, suicidally.

John Belushi demonstrated that there is nothing remotely glamorous about killing yourself with drugs. In his better moments, such as at a small gathering in his penthouse at L.A.'s Chateau Marmont Hotel, he was merely disgusting. Bob Woodward describes this scene in *Wired:* "John was . . . blowing his nose a lot and as usual tossing the used tissue on the floor. One time he hit his manager's wife, Deborah, on the shoe." At his worst, as in one postmidnight New York drug buy, he was a hollowed-out container for drugs, a coke junkie. "Bear had a lot of cocaine at his place that night . . . piled in one big mound in the kitchen. Pullis bought a gram for $120. He also noticed that John was scooping some into a small plastic bag while Bear was out of the room. . . . There was no longer anything recreational or social about John's cocaine use."

Like many hopeless romantics, John was fascinated with heroin. Heroin was the drug of Ray Charles, Keith Richards, Billie Holliday, John Coltrane, and William Burroughs. Heroin, he had heard, was the ultimate stone. The perils of addiction probably only made it more appealing, a potential macho contest: Belushi vs. heroin. If you could beat heroin—and hadn't Keith and Brother Ray?—you could beat anything and anyone. You were a *true* bad ass—up there, in fact, *with* Brother Ray and Keith.

Belushi talked about heroin sometimes, expressing his fascination at odd moments and with characteristic infantile bravado. One day he walked into his accountant's office and started talking about it. Writes Woodward, " 'I have a lot of friends who are doing heroin,' he said, the accountant's assistant recalled. 'I don't think I could ever do heroin. If I did, I'd have a very hard time stopping—if ever.' " Another time, Belushi inquired of the author and former Washington hostess Barbara Howar, who had become a confidante: "Have you ever tied off?" When Howar said no, John assured her, "It's like kissing God." But at this point his boast was probably just wishful thinking.

If he had on occasion tried shooting coke, the condition of his nose, repeatedly treated by an L.A. doctor, confirmed that mostly he snorted it. At the same time, while he may have tried heroin, snorting or shooting it, his naiveté about it in the weeks preceding his death suggests strongly that he was mostly inexperienced, both in the drug and in the mainline method.

Though some peripheral people claimed otherwise, his partner, the forthright Dan Aykroyd, said no way. "People, the man who grasped me, danced with me, met my eye, and planned the future was not a junkie. As a prop, the hypo made us laugh. It was not a tool in his life. . . . The John I knew could only have been assisted into oblivion during the course of an experiment. He hated needles and could never have inserted a hypo into himself. He wasn't that good a mechanic.'' And though one is inclined to believe Aykroyd, the record shows that in the 24 hours immediately prior to his death, during the course of what Aykroyd terms his "experiment," John Belushi was injected by hypo at least 24 times—for a mind-boggling average of a shot an hour.

The last few days Judy and John spent together, his last few days in New York, were rocky, as recounted in *Wired*. At one point, waking up from a midday nap after an all-nighter on the town, John started coughing. "He sounded like a drowning man, and he was spitting up blood," said Judy. He wanted to know what was wrong with him, and Judy assured him he was doing it to himself. "I'm out of control," said Belushi, to which his wife agreed.

"Then he went back to sleep, to wake up a few hours later.

" 'What did I take?' he asked. 'Heroin?' "

Woodward continues, "For an instant, this struck Judy as funny, and she had to laugh. . . . On top of everything else, it was too disturbing to think about. She knew he had almost a romantic notion about heroin—the great forbidden, the drug of last resort."

John Belushi arrived back in Los Angeles the evening of February 28, 1982, checked into a bungalow at the Chateau Marmont, and went out looking for trouble. He was supposed to be in L.A. working on the rewrite of his and Don Novello's script for a romantic comedy called *Noble Rot*, for which John, as writer and star, would be paid close to $2 million. Instead, at the house of a friend and sometime dealer, he met up with a thirty-five-year-old show-biz marginal named Cathy Smith, who at that moment was shooting herself up with heroin. Saying he'd done it before in New York, John of course wanted to try. He asked for a speedball, a coke–smack combo, and Smith gave it to him. "Hey, I like it," Woodward quotes him as saying. "It feels great." With a man as compulsive as Belushi, you could probably have predicted the rest.

John Belushi spent the next four days of his life mostly hanging around with Cathy Smith, snorting heroin, shooting heroin, shooting speedballs, snorting and shooting coke, drinking, and mostly never sleeping. He was upset because the studio didn't like his coked-up first draft for *Noble Rot*. On March 4, he called Judy for sympathy and said he was going to return to New York the next night on the red-eye. Judy sensed his desperate condition and called Smokey Wendell, who agreed to get back on the case the next day. After receiving a call from John and consulting with Judy, Dan Aykroyd agreed to fly to L.A. the next day to try to retrieve his partner. In the meantime, between calls for sympathy, John and Cathy continued their danse macabre.

Around two o'clock on the morning of Friday, March 5, John and Smith and a writer friend of John's, Nelson Lyon, were heading back to his bungalow at the Chateau from the VIP On The Rox club when John made Smith pull over. John puked. When Smith asked him what was wrong, he blamed it on a greasy dinner. They got back to the bungalow, and as arranged earlier in the evening, Robin Williams stopped by. Woodward writes: "John stood up and got out some cocaine, and Williams had a little. Then John sat down and his head just dropped, as if he had fallen asleep or passed out. In about five seconds he lifted his head.

" 'What's up?' Williams asked. . . . 'Are you okay?'

" 'Yeah,' John said distractedly. 'Took a couple of 'ludes.' " He sat there on the verge of sleep.

"Williams decided it was time to go. . . . "

Robert DeNiro then stopped by, had a snort of coke, told Judy later that he found Smith "trashy" and John "strung out" and left around three in the morning. Shortly thereafter, John shooed off Nelson Lyon, who was feeling pretty sickly anyway from the massive quantities of drugs, and Smith and Belushi were alone.

As reconstructed by the police and biographer Woodward, the next few hours went something like this: John said he felt cold and asked Smith to stick around. He also asked her if she had any more coke. Even Smith had some sense of limits. "You haven't had any sleep for days," she told Belushi. "Why don't you go to sleep?" Belushi didn't listen, however, and now pulled out one last packet of his own coke. Dutifully, Cathy Smith mixed it with some smack and gave herself a shot and then John. The two then took showers and, with Smith wearing John's jogging suit, they sat on the bed and talked, mostly about John's forthcoming movie deals. Smith tried coming on to John, but he wasn't interested. He said he felt cold again. Smith told him to get under the covers, adding, "I'll turn up the heat."

Cathy Smith went in the front room of the bungalow and started writing a letter, but stopped when she heard wheezing coming from Belushi. She checked him, asking if he was all right. He said he was, and then she brought him a glass of water. When she said she was going to get something to eat, he said, "Don't leave," and then turned over and went back to sleep. Smith ordered room service and signed Belushi's name for it around eight o'clock. Around ten, she gathered up her syringe and her spoon, checked on John, who was snoring, and borrowed his car for the ride to the Santa Monica Boulevard bar where she placed horse bets.

Four hours later, she returned. It was all over. Police took Cathy Smith into custody at the scene, and a few minutes later a gurney with what looked like a whale aboard was wheeled out of the bungalow on its way to the morgue. Belushi's karate trainer had found the body and had tried to revive it and had refused to believe it was dead. It was. And the coroner found a big, fatty heart—indicating not an enlarged capacity for sentiment, but incipient high blood pressure—and a swollen brain; he later ruled that "John Belushi, a thirty-three-year-old white male, died of acute toxicity from cocaine and heroin."

John Belushi had finally arrived. Now he was a certifiably dead rock 'n' roll star.

17
BOB MARLEY
Exodus

There is no name in this book more closely linked with drugs than that of Bob Marley, and yet there was no man further removed from the conventional, sixties-style drug culture. His name is as synonymous with marijuana as Cheech & Chong's—yet no one in the pop-cultural realm was taken more seriously than Bob Marley. He was an outlaw, but he was awarded Jamaica's Order of Merit, and when he died—not of drugs—his body lay in state in the National Heroes Arena in Kingston, eulogized by the prime minister. He was a musician. But for Jamaicans, and for much of the dark-skinned Third World, he was also a prophet. He was a man, but spoke the words of God. And, as perhaps one would have to be to enclose such paradox and range, he was a mystery.

He was born Robert Nesta Marley at 2:30 A.M. on February 6 (or thereabouts; neither he nor his mother was ever sure of the date), 1945, in the town of Rhoden Hall, in St. Ann's Parish, Jamaica. He was the son of Cedella Malcolm, a nineteen-year-old black woman, and Captain Norval Sinclair Marley, a middle-aged white man. Though Captain Marley did marry Cedella Malcolm, in 1944, to legitimize their coming child, he broke a promise to take care of the two after that, and Cedella was forced to move back in with her father, a merchant and farmer. Life with father, however, was no carefree idyll. All members of the family were expected to contribute to the general good by working in his fields, and home for Cedella and Robert—or Nesta, as his family called him—was a one-room hilltop shack. Finally, when he was fourteen, his mother took Nesta to the big city, Kingston, where there was better schooling and ultimately, she hoped, a better life.

At school, Nesta learned Jamaican history. He learned about the slave forefathers of Jamaican blacks, about oppression, and about rebellion. The 1950s were still a time of oppression in Jamaica, and once more rebellion against British rule was brewing. Marley liked history. He could relate to it. In the Trench Town ghetto, the ancient currents rose up to smite him every day, and Marley was learning to smite back. To his mother's chagrin, her Nesta was becoming a street fighter and a talker of ghetto slang, a rude boy. He was also becoming entranced by the sound-system men whose record players and public-address systems blasted syncopated ska music throughout the ghetto. Finally, he told his mother he wanted to be called Bob.

Bob Marley decided to try his hand at singing and songwriting. Jimmy Chambers, a friend (later better known as Jimmy Cliff), introduced the seventeen-year-old Marley to producer Leslie Kong. Hard up for product, Kong agreed to record Marley performing his song "Judge Not" and to pay the youngster £20 (then about $40) and two free copies of the record. When the teenage Bob left the studio, according to biographer Timothy White, he was "on Marcus Garvey Drive, headed back to Trench Town clutching two black vinyl platters in thick gray cardboard sleeves, with two ten-pound notes pushed deep into the pockets of his baggy trousers. Every hundred yards or so, he pulled the gleaming platters halfway out of their sleeves and giggled. . . . Each time he looked at the records the sight of them made him quicken his pace. . . .

"He was at the corner of First Street and Central Road when it hit him: he didn't know a soul who owned a phonograph."

Kong recorded Marley several more times in 1962, to little acclaim, and finally the two split up, Bob angrily accusing the producer of welshing on a payment. The experience had convinced Marley that music was his way out of Trench Town, and in 1963 he enlisted childhood friends Bunny Livingston and Peter Tosh, found a new producer, and put together the Wailers.

In the summer of 1962, Jamaica gained its independence from

Britain, which brought as many problems as it solved. Having won their fight against colonial domination, Jamaicans now had no one left to fight but themselves. In Trench Town, the situation was extremely volatile. The ghetto, and the rude boys in particular, was simmering. Like the Beatles in the U.S. and U.K., the Wailers had arrived at the right place at the right time, in a well-stoked Jamaica at a moment of change, and they addressed that place and moment directly, in a way no Jamaican musical group had ever done.

"Simmer Down" hit number one on the island's charts in February 1964. As Tim White writes, "Bob had composed the tune in response to his mother's concern that he was keeping company with young thugs and ruffians; his intensity as he sang the lyric sprang as much from his irritation with (and his desire to prove himself to) his parent as from any particular desire to offer a warning to the island's jaunty juvenile delinquents." Standing out from the standard Jamaican pop record, the song stood out no less from the run of topical songwriting in Jamaica. " 'Simmer Down' was something quite new: music of the sufferah, a crude, spontaneous volley from the psychic depths of the Dungle underclass [Dungle being the cardboard shantytown built around a Jamaican city dump, whose inhabitants were the untouchables of the Caribbean]."

White continues, "Most significant of all, the shanty-dwellers were addressing their own kind. That they were telling them to watch their step . . . was perhaps laudatory, but the language used was the 'jargon of the gutter.' . . . It was like having some half-naked old cartman projecting his lowly mutterings over the garden wall—with a public-address system!"

Indeed, selling a lot of records and going number one was one thing, but "Simmer Down" instantly meant a lot more. "Reaction in the gutter itself," biographer White concludes, "was roughly akin to what might attend a hail of thunderbolts: a communal shock of self-recognition."

The Wailers continued as one of Jamaica's most popular groups for the next two years, alternating political singles with more conventional doo-wop or Motown-style R & B. The group was yet to play its own instruments, though, functioning solely as a vocal quintet with backup musicians. Then in 1966, discovering they were more or less broke, having been paid almost no royalties, the Wailers disbanded. Marley, recently married to singer Rita Anderson, left Jamaica to find his fortune in the Promised Land of Wilmington, Delaware, U.S.A., where his mother had relocated with relatives three years before.

In Wilmington, Bob worked as a waiter and then at the local Chrysler plant. At night, lonely and alienated, he honed his songwriting craft, writing sophisticated, polished lyrics and melodies. Finally, after almost a year in America, Bob Marley received a draft notice from the U.S. Selective Service and decided to get out of the Promised Land while he still could. Back in Jamaica, where his old producer had continued to issue Wailers singles, which somewhat maintained the band's popularity (while still not paying royalties), Marley rounded up Tosh and Livingston.

During Bob's absence, the Ethiopian emperor Haile Selassie had visited Jamaica, in 1966, and Rita Marley had converted to the millenarian Rastafarian cult. The Rastas believed that Selassie was the Messiah and marijuana a sacrament. Their initiates wore their hair in long, matted braids known as dreadlocks. More and more, Bob noticed, Trench Town rude boys were also sporting dreadlocks and the once secretive Rasta cult seemed to be coming out into the open. Inspired by Rita's enthusiastic preaching, Marley—who had once joked that Rastas in their locks looked like Alfalfa from the Little Rascals—decided to pay a visit to a wise Rasta elder named Planno. Planno reasoned with Bob and interpreted his dreams and took him to a Grounation, the Rasta mass. When Marley finally came down from Planno's mountaintop, he had seen Jah's light.

One more key element fell into place in 1969 when the Wailers connected with producer Lee "Scratch" Perry. Perry stripped them of all vestiges of their doo-wop past, got them to play their own instruments rather than merely front a backup band, and encouraged Aston and Carlton Barrett from his own studio group to join them. Perry emphasized intensity over polish, authenticity over technique.

Perry turned the Wailers into a rock band—albeit a distinctly *Jamaican* rock band, playing distinctly *Jamaican* reggae, the more driving, guitar-oriented syncopated style that had now supplanted the rock-steady style (which had supplanted the oompah, horn-oriented ska). Perry was not a Svengali; for all his meddling, like any good producer he mostly just helped the Wailers become themselves. That is why it worked and kept on working long after Scratch Perry had departed the scene.

The new, stripped-down Wailers were a revelation to listeners old and new. Following the first two Perry-produced albums, *Soul Rebels* and *Soul Revolution,* after three years of obscurity, the band was back on top of the Jamaican pops. At the same time, outside interest was growing. Anticipating the next sensation, the American singer Johnny Nash recorded three Marley songs for his next album and hired the band to do much of the instrumental backing.

Nash's manager arranged for a modest Wailers tour of Britain, in hopes of attracting a major-label record deal. With Marley also working on a soundtrack for a proposed Nash movie and the Wailers records still moving back home, the stage seemed set for big money and international fame. Suddenly, it all began to unravel, and the Wailers found themselves stranded without plane fare in a cold-water flat in London. Enter Chris Blackwell.

Chris Blackwell was the white owner and guiding light behind Island Records. A sometime resident of Jamaica, he had already licensed some of the Wailers' singles for the U.K. market when a middleman approached and explained the band's situation. They wanted a $15,000 advance to record a new album back in Jamaica. And though, as Tim White says, "Blackwell had heard that Bob and his boys were a contrary crew at best," he bought the deal. The album for Island was finished in the winter of 1972, but with numerous last-minute legal encumbrances to be overcome, wasn't released until '73. It was called *Catch a Fire,* which is exactly what the Wailers had done. The record was angry, melodic, direct, political, religious. And it rocked like crazy—that is, you could dance to it. The puzzle was complete: The Wailers had truly become themselves.

The now-classic *Catch a Fire,* which included Bob's own version of his "Stir It Up" as well as the single "Concrete Jungle," sold only moderately well. But it alerted white critics, musicians, and other mainstream pop tastemakers outside Jamaica to be on the lookout for reggae, for a great new band, and for an extraordinary singer and songwriter named Bob Marley. Blackwell, trying to build on this word-of-mouth momentum, promptly put up for more studio time back in Jamaica. By the end of 1973, the Wailers had produced *Burnin'.* With its back-cover photo of a dreadlocked Marley "drawing on a spliff as big as an ice cream cone," and with such tunefully inciteful songs as "I Shot the Sheriff" and "Get Up, Stand Up," *Burnin'* became a true cultural event. By the time Eric Clapton's cover of "I Shot the Sheriff" went to number one in America in the summer of '74, the Wailers had become the rage of rock society and the terror of the tabloids. Tim White chronicles the press reaction. "The American press . . . now began running long, detailed pieces on this Jamaican cult that salaamed in front of icons of an Ethiopian despot and smoked more pot than the populations of Haight-Ashbury and Greenwich Village combined.

"Jamaican society unfolded the *Gleaner* [Kingston's daily paper] . . . one morning to realize that a Rastafarian had suddenly become one of the best-known figures in the Third World . . . a sufferah. . . . the product of the dalliance of a horny white captain in the West India Regiment and a bungo-bessy from the bush."

Over the course of the next half dozen years and nine albums, that rude boy Rasta sufferah would sell well over $200 million worth of records and play to sellout crowds all over the world— drawing more than 100,000 people to one stadium date in Italy! He was an international musical figure of the first order, on a level with the Stones, Stevie Wonder, even the Beatles.

But because of the words he sang and the convictions he maintained, because of his proud proclamation of his non-Christian, black nationalist Rastafarian beliefs and his dreadlocks, and because of his open smoking of marijuana, he was a political figure, too. And because his politics came all wrapped up in his personal charm and was couched in terms of divine enlightenment, he was potentially a very powerful politician. Jamaican plantation owners, who for so long had profited from the island's cheap labor and plentiful natural resources, were not only offended by this sufferah, they were afraid of him.

Nineteen seventy-six was an election year in Jamaica, and people were watching Bob Marley. In June, due to an upsurge in political violence, the governor-general put the island under martial law. But this did not prevent enforcers, representing various factions, from visiting Marley at his Island House headquarters and attempting some not-so-subtle intimidation. Indeed, the situation in Jamaica by November, a month before the elections, was well beyond the control of the police and army, and so Prime Minister Michael Manley called on the one man who might be able to help: Bob Marley. The idea was for the Wailers to perform a free stadium concert on December 5. The event was supposed to "keep de lid on till de election on December 16." There was to be no politics involved, Manley's representative promised. But as Marley well knew, how could there not be?

To some, agreeing to do the concert was a tacit endorsement by Marley of the Manley government, toward which he had shown subtle sympathy in the past. To everyone, even Manley, Marley's agreement to do the concert was dangerous. But Bob acquiesced. A week before the show, now called the Smile Jamaica Festival, a heavily armed vigilante group from Manley's party went on round-the-clock guard at Island House. That night, around quarter of nine, in a scene right out of a Hollywood western, a Marley associate happened to look up from his chores and out the window and noticed that Manley's armed guard was gone. Tim White describes the scene:

"Bob was in the kitchen . . . swallowing a sweet-sour segment of grapefruit when a dull *crack* caused him to drop the fruit. That was when Don Taylor, who had been walking toward Bob and chatting, felt the bullets entering the backs of his legs. . . .

"It was 9:12 P.M. when a rifle-wielding assailant jumped back through the kitchen pantry.

" 'Did you get him?' shouted an armed confederate. . . .

" 'Yeah!' he said. 'I shot him!'

"Don Taylor lay in a heap on the kitchen floor, bleeding internally and externally. . . . He was unaware that because of his casual proximity to his employer he had shielded him . . . and thus saved Bob Marley's life."

Bob Marley's life was not out of danger, though. As it turned out, a total of seven assassins had descended on Island House. Two of them shot Rita as she tried to escape with the Marley children. Another, barely sixteen, closed his eyes and fired repeatedly into the band's rehearsal room. Still another went to the kitchen to make sure the main job had been done. White continues, "The gunman got off eight shots. The last creased Marley's breast below his heart and went clean through his arm." And then, again just as in the movies, a police car happened by on a routine patrol, and the band of assassins scattered.

Four were injured in the raid, including Rita Marley, who had a bullet removed from beneath her scalp, and Bob, who was treated for flesh wounds. But all, including Don Taylor and the other, more seriously injured Marley friend, survived. They were saved by the police, by the relative ineptitude of the assassins, and, Bob and the others believed (and well they might), by Jah. Jah had plans for Bob Marley.

After much soul-searching at a secret mountain hideout established for him by Michael Manley, and over the trepidations of family and band, the still-bandaged Marley made the courageous decision that the Smile Jamaica show must go on. Not only were the assassins still on the loose, but it was uncertain who they were. Presumably they weren't sent by Manley's party. But were they sent by the Manley administration's police acting autonomously? Were they sent by the CIA, who had an interest in keeping Cuban sympathizer Manley out of a second term? Were they the opposition party? Renegades in the opposition? Or were they just gangsters with an apolitical motive? Not knowing who they were—and at the same time knowing that any one of the suspects would be a formidable foe—made it all that much harder to ensure Marley's safety at the big, outdoor concert.

Still, Marley played, and his power and presence were increased a hundredfold. The prophet had now walked through fire. He showed the audience his wounds, and then as White says, "The last thing they saw before the reigning King of Reggae disappeared back into the hills was the image of the man mimicking the two-pistol fast draw of a frontier gunslinger, his locks thrown back in triumphant laughter." Two weeks later, Michael Manley won the election.

Two years later, truly a world figure and Jamaica's greatest hero, Marley again performed a concert to bring the island together and to quell violence. According to representatives from *both* major parties, who approached him together, Marley may even have prevented a bloody civil war. If in the end it didn't completely stop the political violence, the One Love Peace Festival on April 22, 1978, did help establish the new Jamaican peace movement. It also created an impossible moment when Bob Marley somehow got Michael Manley and Edward Seaga onstage together to shake hands. Marley's magic and legend were once again reaffirmed.

What had Jah saved Bob Marley for? we might ask bitterly (though Bob Marley probably wouldn't). He survived the violent politics of Jamaica, performing yet another benefit, this time for Jamaican children, in 1979. He survived a disillusioning 1980 trip to Africa, where he performed as part of the new nation of Zimbabwe's official independence celebration and, after being inadvertently teargassed, realized that the new boss in that tormented country would likely be much the same as the old. He survived the Jamaican music business and not receiving his royalties. He broke through the narrow-minded American music business, maintaining his integrity in Babylon. He survived the smothering attention of the worldwide media and being kissed by Bianca Jagger at a black-tie reception in Paris. He survived the departure from the band of childhood pals Tosh and Livingston. And he survived the American quasi-Rasta hustlers who began to surround him, to suck him dry. Can it be then that Jah preserved

him through all this so that Bob Marley might finally be killed by
soccer? Jah know, one supposes, Jah know.

Bob Marley was a soccer freak. He played the game, and well,
every day, at home or on tour. The first injury to his right big toe
occurred in 1976 when he caught it on a rusty nail while playing
on the Boys' Town field in Jamaica. It healed, but then in May
1977, playing soccer while on tour in France, he reinjured the
toe, tearing the nail off. When the wound hadn't healed by July,
an Island Records functionary took Bob to a London doctor.
After several visits, during which the bad wound only grew
worse, the doctor told Marley the toe would have to be ampu-
tated. On religious grounds, Marley turned down the recommen-
dation and then found a more amenable surgeon in Miami,
Florida, who performed a skin graft, which he told Marley had
been a success. Nevertheless, not long thereafter, the thirty-
three-year-old Marley had intimations of his mortality. "Me
gwan die at t'irty-six," he told them, "jus' like Christ."

The toe bothered him again in Zimbabwe, the surgeon's
pronouncement aside. But on the next leg of the tour, in New
York City, he began to feel a more general malaise. During his
Madison Square Garden concert, he almost passed out onstage,
and the next day, while running with a friend in Central Park,
Bob collapsed. After being taken to a doctor by the friend, he
managed to make it to the next date, in Pittsburgh. There he
informed Rita, who had gone on ahead, of the diagnosis. The toe
had evidently become cancerous and had spread mutant cells
throughout his system. "Doctor seh brain tumor black me out,"
Bob Marley now told his wife.

After barely making it through the Pittsburgh concert, Bob
finally agreed, at Rita's insistence, to cancel his tour and begin
the desperate, demoralizing tour of medical science and quackery
familiar to many cancer patients and their families. First, to
Memorial Sloan-Kettering Cancer Center in New York, where
word leaked out about his illness, further demoralizing Bob.
Next, to a friendly doctor in Miami. Next, to the Mexican cancer
clinic where Steve McQueen had gone. Back to Sloan-Kettering,
where it was reported that he was allowed to use marijuana

legally for the first time in order to erase the discomfort of radiation therapy, which had also caused him to lose his famous hair.

By November 1980, Bob Marley was not expected to live out the year. Cancer had been detected in his liver and lungs, as well as in his brain. Finally, at the suggestion of a Jamaican doctor, he traveled to Bavaria to the "whole-body" clinic of a physician named Josef Issels, whose nutritionally based therapy was said to work wonders. Some say it did. "Issels managed to keep Bob Marley alive more than six months longer than any other doctor would dare to even project," writes Tim White. But eventually Issels gave up.

On May 9, 1981, Marley flew back to Miami, where his mother was waiting for him. "Maddah, don' cry," he said to Cedella. "I'll be all right. I'm gwan to prepare a place." On May 11, 1981, Bob Marley flew back to Jah.

18

KAREN CARPENTER

No More Songs About Buildings and Food

*W*e've only just begun."

It was her most famous song, her theme song. But it might be the theme song for any of the tragically abbreviated lives in this book. Indeed, and all the young dudes in rock 'n' roll heaven might gladly welcome it as such (everyone loves to have a theme song), if it just weren't so damned insipid.

There's the rub. In a thirty-year-old musical form that's been shot through with insipid singers and their insipid songs—from Pat Boone and "April Love" to David Crosby and "Almost Cut My Hair" to Olivia Newton-John and everything she ever did (except "Physical")—you could still say with a reasonable degree of certainty that Karen Carpenter takes the cake (I mean figuratively, of course). And you could say that the most interesting, the *only* commanding, thing Karen Carpenter ever did was die.

But (for rock 'n' roll) what an original way to go! I mean, there have been skinny rock stars. In fact, since Keith Richards there *mostly* have been skinny rock stars. While all of them probably get into some pretty heavy starvation action before the album-cover photo session or the tour, Karen Carpenter was the only one to actually starve herself to *death*.

What's truly commanding and compelling about Karen's death is not so much that it's unique in rock, but that it's *not* unique in the society outside. Karen Carpenter succumbed to an illness that is both common among young American women (at least in its incipient stages) and pathetically symptomatic of their plight in our culture. While heavy-metal rock stars act out the aggressive, macho fantasies of the boys in the rock 'n' roll audience, Karen Carpenter lived out the passive, "feminine" fantasies of the girls. As it turned out, for all the gloom-and-doom mongering of the boys, it was much more lethal to play the *femme*.

At least it was for Karen Carpenter, dead at thirty-two.

In the age of the jogger, when the whole world seems to have gone crazy for surfaces, when it's a sin to be fat, for boys and girls alike, maybe telling her short story one more time is not simply gratuitous violence.

"Karen had been a little overweight as a teenager," brother Richard told *People* magazine. "She loved tacos and chili. But—to us, she wasn't that fat. When she was seventeen, she went on the Stillman Diet . . . and lost between twenty and twenty-five pounds. She was at her best weight—between 115 and 120—until 1975, when the illness first became serious."

From Tom Nolan's 1974 *Rolling Stone* profile of the Carpenters, a hint: "At a back table in Beverly Hills' La Scala restaurant . . . while everyone else at dinner (including her brother) was enjoying sumptuous pasta, [Karen] had before her a simple green salad and iced tea. She was, as usual, on a diet."

Richard continues. "That year [1975] we had to cancel a European tour because her weight was way down.... She was exhausted.... Finally, she went into the hospital for five days of bed rest and then spent almost two months in bed at our parents'.

"It was right around that time that we heard about anorexia...."

Karen once described an encounter with a radio interviewer. And perhaps dropped another hint: "This DJ from Toronto called me up on the air.... He opens up by saying, 'What's the difference between you and Paul and Paula?' 'There were two of them. There's two of us,' I said. 'That's where it ends.' 'OK,' he says, 'what about Sonny and Cher?' ... 'She's thinner.'"

Later she commiserated with Richard, who was bemoaning the latest hardships of the road: "'Boy, there've been a lot of firsts on this tour,' [Richard] said. 'No grapefruit yesterday, no ice cream the day before....'

"*'No vanilla ice cream,'* Karen said with wonderment. 'I almost died when I heard that one.'"

Richard continues: "From early 1975 on I tried every method I knew to get her to eat.... Karen was always worried about the way she looked, so I tried to appeal to that. I told her she was too thin and that people were noticing it. And that she wouldn't be able to continue our schedule if she didn't get more fuel. Although her voice was never affected, you could hear gasps from the audience when she came onstage...." Eventually, Karen herself admitted she needed help and went into psychiatric therapy in New York for nine months, but to no avail. As a last resort, she was checked into Manhattan's Lenox Hill Hospital and force-fed.

"We all went down to see her in the hospital. She had been down to 80 pounds, and she was about 110 when she came home to L.A. for Thanksgiving 1982, when we had turkey and all the trimmings. She was definitely improved, but there were signs that she wasn't 100 percent turned around—she was picking at food, and there were certain rituals in eating....

"There never was a point where she acted like she was sick. She was her bubbly, energetic self right to the end, and she ate well in her last weeks. . . . [After the Grammy awards] I took her to St. Germain for dinner. She had an appetizer, French bread, wine, and entree and everything that came with it. I knew she had gotten an urge for tacos earlier and that she was eating chili again—one of her favorites."

Yet, less than two months later, on February 4, 1983, thirty-two-year-old Karen Carpenter died in her sleep at her parents' house. Primary cause: heart attack. Secondary cause: long-term effects of anorexia nervosa, the fashion disease.

19

ELVIS PRESLEY

Rust Never Sleeps

I was once in the same room with Elvis Presley. The year was 1972. The room, however, was Madison Square Garden.

It was the first time Elvis had played New York, and although I wasn't a stone freak for the dude—the Elvis my generation knew mostly performed schlock in Las Vegas—I *was* a rock 'n' roller and recognized him as my king. Up in the cheap seats, behind a lady with a lacquered beehive hairdo and a squirming facsimile of Claud Aikens for a husband, all you could really hear was a dull, jet-engine roar—35 singers and musicians playing 100-decibel sympho-billy pop through a reverb box and the house PA system in a 20,000-seat, concrete hockey rink. All you could really see was a tiny doll in a white jumpsuit with a gigantic collar (suddenly, you understood the collar!), even through Beehive's binoculars. It took five minutes to recognize "Hound Dog" through the acoustical glossolalia, by which time Elvis had segued into another hit you couldn't recognize ("Is that 'Love Me Tender' or 'Jailhouse Rock?'"), and on into another, and so on.

Just when you thought he was looking straight at you—and *waving* ("He noticed! He noticed!")—he turned around to face the audience again, and you realized that he had been conducting,

and looking at, the band. I've seen plenty of concerts in Madison Square Garden, and it's never real good. But with Elvis it was never worse. Where some artists can actually make a hockey rink seem small and intimate, Elvis Presley made the Garden seem even larger and more impersonal. Still, I was once in the same room with Elvis Presley, and that, as Elvis himself may have understood, was the whole point of the exercise anyway.

Maybe it goes back to something the critic Greil Marcus said. "Elvis," said Marcus, who loved the man as much as any beehived New Jersey hillbilly, "transcends his talent to the point of dispensing with it altogether. Performing a kind of enormous victory rather than winning it, Elvis strides the boards with such glamour, such magnetism, that he allows his audience to transcend their desire for his talent. Action is irrelevant when one can simply delight in the presence of a man who has made history, and who has triumphed over it."

There is something still poignant in the Elvis Presley story. It lies somewhere between the *Enquirer* headlines that announce, "Elvis Has Spoken to Me from Beyond the Grave" ("Elvis is now reunited with his mother and brother and he's truly at peace. . . .") and Albert Goldman's contemptuous biography, between the cultists who have their faces surgically altered in the Rock 'n' Roll Messiah's image and the assassins who would make of Elvis a fat, clammy picture of decadence, a "junkie" and a "pervert" (to quote Goldman's sanctimony), ultimately an insignificance, a clown. It lies in the fact that, unlike other of the great modern artists, Picasso, say, or even John Lennon, Elvis remained one of us. It was almost as if the Fates had gotten the wrong guy.

He was a lazy man of no deep, shining intelligence, whose accomplishments, like his sultry good looks, were basically an accident of birth, almost entirely the result of innate talent rather than conscious artifice. Where John Lennon could explore and develop his innate talent and so make a life of art, Elvis's talent hung there like a third arm (to expropriate Edward Albee's imagery), a somewhat embarrassing appendage of mysterious origin that had somehow gotten him to where he was.

Which is not to say that Elvis didn't want to be the King. He did, badly. "I was the hero of the comic book," he would tell his minions. "I saw movies and I was the hero of the movie. So every dream I ever dreamed has come true a hundred times." In dreaming of glory (and then never doubting its rewards, believing that the dreams had come true, a hundred wonderful times over) and in wanting to be king, he was all the more the commoner. In every link of gold chain he lay around his neck, in every acre of Naugahyde that covered his house and airplane, in every 4:00 A.M. feast and every pound of flesh it added, in his gang of guys and the rented-amusement-park parties, in the nine Lincolns purchased in one evening, in the Cadillacs given away to strangers, in every little happy pill, he was one of us: basically lazy, basically stupid, basically hedonistic, basically—and poignantly—fallible. Now, who would have done it differently?

Who *could* have done it differently? Elvis Presley is a picture of me and you if *we* had gotten what we dreamed. No doubt that was part of his appeal. It is also, no doubt, why some fans, the cultists, identify with him so completely, so psychotically. It is part of why others prefer to heap upon him contempt and derision, envy and fear. If other performers have had the common touch, Elvis was so effective because he was simply common, without the distance.

I thought of all this when I looked at a picture of the latter-day Elvis in one of his big-collared shirts—not his stage gear, but the street clothing—and realized how much he looked like my big brother. My brother had grown up on him and with him and had also gotten fat and loved his big-collar shirts, which he also pulled out over the lapels of his jacket. Elvis was just a Joe who was trying to look cool by the same standards that my brother was trying to look cool. When big collars were in, Elvis wore big collars. When long hair was in, even Elvis let his greasy hair go natural and a little shaggy, just like my bro. The guy was not above it. In fact, he was beneath it, as subject to the dictates of the mysterious Them as my fat, jolly, ex-greaser, hedonist, big-collared bro.

I said at the beginning of this book that these people, these rock stars, objects of our dreams and fantasies, represent something of the way we all live—and die. I didn't recognize then that none does so more than Elvis. I would have picked John Lennon, because he's the one I loved best. I now understand that we are not necessarily who we love. And where I started out chortling over Elvis Presley's excesses, I now realize that I am laughing nervously.

Which is not to say I shouldn't. Which is not to say that it isn't damn funny sometimes. Aren't you?

If I had a jillion dollars, what would *I* do?

Albert Goldman describes Elvis's fantasies. "What [Elvis] sought as his erotic goal was a group of girls who would agree to strip down to their panties and wrestle with each other while Elvis stared. . . . In fact, with the fine focus characteristic of his kind [perverts], what Elvis described as his ultimate fulfillment was not the sight of the girls or even the crotch but the vision of black pubic hairs protruding around the edges of white panties. . . .

"If Elvis became sufficiently aroused by the spectacle . . . he might go down on a girl or dry hump her. . . . If Elvis were feeling particularly daring, he might allow a girl to jack him off."

If *I* were twenty years old and had a jillion dollars . . .

Red West on Elvis: "When he took over the house on Perugia Way [in Los Angeles] he had two big mirrors installed . . . one-way mirrors. . . . He had one of the mirrors in a closet that looked into a bedroom. Now whenever any guy was making out with a chick in this bedroom Elvis and all of us would rush in and see the action. . . . There was another mirror in the dressing room of the pool house that he had installed, and he could watch the girls getting undressed when they were changing to go into the pool."

If I had a jillion dollars . . .

Albert Goldman describes Elvis's airplane. "Elvis likes to boast that he is the only entertainer ever to own for his personal use a four-engine jet airliner...a Convair 880 that had carried ninety-six passengers when it was owned by Delta Airlines....

"The forward cabin is a very plushy...club room, furnished with two long curving bench sofas covered with fat cushions of crushed velour...some card tables, leather lounge chairs, TV monitors, and a fifteen-thousand-dollar quadrophonic sound system.

"Behind this room is the dining-conference room, which is furnished with six huge leather spaceman chairs ranged along either side of a surfboard-shaped Danish modern table with a green leather surface and a teak rim. Meals served on this spiffy board are framed with silverware bearing Elvis's personal monogram....

"The most important compartment is, of course, the bedroom.... [It] is decorated entirely in shades of restful blue: royal blue for the carpeting, which runs up to the windowsills, pale blue for the huge velvet bedspread; royal blue again for the suede headboard. At the end of the bed is the TV.... Finally, there is a bathroom....

"Picture a plastic bathroom counter in a shade of brilliant lapis lazuli with a canary-yellow sink. Atop the sink is an ornately patterned, gold-plated nozzle and faucet fixture, whose handles are real lapis.... With this assemblage of precious metal, semiprecious stone and cheap plastic...you have the epitome of the king's taste." (Blue is *my* favorite color, too!)

If a had a jillion , maybe I'd give some away....

Red West recalls Elvis's generosity. "Dave Hebler remembers a day...when Presley suddenly slapped him on the back and said, 'I'm going to buy you and Joe a Maserati each.' ...As it turned out, there were no Maseratis in Memphis...so he piled into a car and headed down to Shilling Motors...where he proceeded to buy no less than nine Lincoln Mark IVs.

"...[Elvis] also bought some Cadillacs that day, although I can't remember how many. What I do remember, however, was this black couple at the Cadillac dealer's.... Anyway, he sees this lady looking at a Cadillac Seville and he strikes up a conversation with her and idly asks, 'Do you like that car?' She replied, 'Oh, yes, it's very nice.' Presley said, 'Fine, pick one out. I'm going to buy one for you.' The lady looked like she was going to faint, but she did pick one out and he did buy it for her.''

He also carried the joke one step further—as I might if I had a jillion. . . .

''When the story hit the wire services, an announcer in Vail, Colorado, reported the story. He signed off the report with a one-liner: 'Elvis, if you're listening, I could use a car myself.' Presley . . . got on the telephone.

'' 'What color do you like?' Presley asked casually. . . . The next day the announcer was driving a new Cadillac.''

If I had a jillion dollars, I might express myself strongly. . . .

West continues, ''Elvis doesn't like too many other singers—at least living ones. . . . He doesn't like competition.

''Worst of all, he really hates Robert Goulet for some reason. I don't remember whether he had ever met him or not or whether he had seen him perform live. Anyway, one afternoon . . . he is eating breakfast and on comes Robert Goulet on the big-screen television set. Very slowly, Elvis finishes what he has in his mouth, puts down his knife and fork, picks up this big mother of a .22 and—boom—blasts old Robert clean off the screen and the television set to pieces.''

If *I* had a jillion and the adoration of the world, I might start believing I was special. . . .

West goes on: ''He firmly believes he has the powers of psychic healing by the laying on of hands. He believes he will be reincarnated. He believes he has the strength of will to move clouds in the air. . . . He firmly believes he is a prophet who was destined to lead, designated by God for a special role in life. . . .

''He used to return to the funeral home where his mother was laid out. . . . I don't mean he would just go there during the day and look around. I mean he would go there at three in the morning and wander around looking at all the embalmed bodies. . . .

''He is telling us all the cosmetic things the morticians do when people are in accidents. He is showing us . . . the jugular veins and things like that. How a body is bled. . . .

And if *I* had boundless fortune and fame, I might even try to get some revenge. . . .

"The man [Elvis] is repeating over and over, 'Mike Stone must die, he must die. You will do it for me, you must, he has no right to live.' . . .

"The man staggers back from inside the closet gripping a gray-green M-16 rifle. Sonny . . . backs toward the door. The man . . . presses the gun into his hand. . . .

" 'He has hurt me so much. . . . He has broken up my family. He has taken my wife from me.'

"Sonny rejected Presley's pleas to kill Mike Stone with horror, but they lay like a festering sore on Red's mind. . . . 'Well, like a big dumb ass, I got a telephone number for a hit.' " (Eventually, Elvis chickened out: "Maybe it's a bit heavy. Just let's leave it off for now.")

If I had a jillion and world adulation and guys who'd kill for me on a whim, I might get a little hard, even mean—for instance, when a groupie interrupted my pool game trying to get her car out of the driveway. . . .

West continues: "[Elvis] took that pool cue in his fist. . . . Then, like he was throwing a spear, he just leaned back and threw it right at her. . . . She had no time to duck. The sharp end of the pool cue bored right into her body. It hit her just above the nipple of the left breast. She didn't scream. It was more like a sharp little gasp, and she crumpled backwards on the floor. . . . "

Said El, "Drag her ass out of here."

If *I* had it all, finally, the American dream on a world-class scale, and never had to worry about losing it, I would *definitely* get high. . . .

West on Elvis's drug abuse: "[Elvis] takes pills to go to sleep. He takes pills to get up. He takes pills to go to the john, and he takes pills to stop him from going to the john. There have been times when he was so hyper on uppers that he has had trouble breathing, and on one occasion he thought he was going to die. His system doesn't work anymore like a normal human being's. The pills do all the work for him. He is a walking pharmaceutical shop. He has smoked marijuana, but he doesn't like to smoke it because it burns his throat. He takes uppers and downers and all sorts of very strong painkillers, Percodan and the stuff they give terminal cancer patients.''

And if I had access to those kinds of pills, I would probably make a mistake. . . .

Albert Goodman describes Elvis's last night. "Elvis changed into a pair of blue pajamas and switched on the big TV facing the bed. He picked up a book on psychic energy but found he was still not inclined to sleep. At six-thirty [in the morning] he called downstairs for his sleeping medication, and Rickey Stanley brought upstairs some Dilaudid. . . .

"Around eight in the morning, Ginger was awakened by Elvis calling downstairs for more sleeping medication. . . . Rickey brought up a standard packet of sleeping pills that included Quaaludes, Seconal, Tuinol, Amytal, Valium, and a couple of Demerol tablets: eight pills in all, a fatal dose for a normal human being but precisely what Elvis took every morning before retiring.

"This morning, apparently, he feared that he would not experience the desired effect because just fifteen minutes after Rickey left his room, Elvis was on the phone to Dr. Nick's [his personal physician] office, where he found Nurse Henley. He explained that he was going to have a trying day. . . . It was vital that he receive some extra sleeping medication. She agreed to help him.

"She called her husband . . . and instructed him to take from the bag of medications . . . two Valmid tablets and a 'Placidyl placebo.' Valmid is a nonbarbiturate hypnotic, and two of those elongated blue pulvules are a standard prescription for insomnia. . . . The drugs were given to Aunt Delta, who brought them up to the bedroom and handed them to Elvis. Receiving these pills was the last act anyone in the group witnessed Elvis perform, save for Ginger.

"GIRL ELVIS WAS GOING TO MARRY TELLS HER HEART-BREAKING STORY—by Ginger Alden.

"I'll never forget his last words: 'Precious, I'm going to go in the bathroom and read.' And I can never forget the horror of finding his body on the floor of his bathroom just hours later, his face purple and his eyes blood-red.''

Born January 8, 1935, in Tupelo, Mississippi, son of a truck driver and a seamtress, Elvis Aaron Presley died August 16, 1977, in Memphis. Cause: heart attack (they say with a straight face).

"I'm not fucked up by no means. On the contrary, I've never been in better condition in my life." (Elvis Presley to Red West in an early-morning phone conversation nine months before Elvis's death.)

I guess I'm just lucky that my dreams never came true, a hundred times.

20

JOHN LENNON

The King Is Gone

*T*he only good thing about not growing old with John Lennon is that we have the whole second half of our lives to get over it. At the same time, the first half is now definitely, irretrievably over.

It's going to *take* half a lifetime. John was my Beatle doll, and I was the eleven-year-old moptop faggot who asked him why parents don't understand and shared my dreams with him and made him a shoebox house in which to live. John was my imaginary friend, big brother, father, platonic lover. He was my hero. He was my king—of rock 'n' roll goes without saying—he was *our* king: King of the Kounterkulture, King of the World. "Whaddya got?" like Brando said. Well, where *I* come from, he was king of it.

Indeed, if in wanting to be King, Elvis became all the more one of us, then in wanting to abdicate, John became king forever. He wasn't one of us. Not after the Beatles and all that they became and implied. He *couldn't* be. For him to believe he was one of us, a commoner again, would have been false modesty, hypocrisy. To keep trying to *be* one of us, however, was part of the quality that had raised him up in the first place: a quality of intelligence and sensitivity—and will—combined with massive talent. Which is not to say he was perfect—who would *want* him perfect? Which is not to say he wasn't sometimes extremely imperfect, wicked, cruel. Yes, he was a sinner. But then they make the best saints.

My fucking mother threw out my Beatle dolls and my collection of Beatles magazines and posters and junk—even my singles. (Goddamn! "She Loves You" on Swan—that's worth *money,* Ma!) Then she called me the day after John was shot to say... well, actually, to say she was sorry. Not about the singles. About our loss. *Our* loss? Yes, she said, she remembered me and Kevin with our Beatles stuff and all and just felt like a whole something bigger had died. Basically, I think she was talking about my childhood, which was *her* (more or less) youth. Still, somewhere, mixed in with the stock Irish morbidity, she shed a few genuine tears for him, too.

So I guess he has a legacy beyond the Swan 45s traded among the clammy palms of the world's rock flea markets, and I guess that legacy would be greater unity, a raised consciousness about peace and nonviolence, a bigger sense of fun and of fairness, a *bridging,* in the end, of the generation gap (along with the bridging in general), love, some great music, some meaningful moments at my shoebox, and 200 million teenage rock bands. Someday maybe I'll be able to appreciate it, if I can ever get through the sadness. For now, I try not to think about John Lennon. In fact, starting to tell his story, I cried. I mean, it's one thing to goof on dead rock stars, but now you're talking about the man I loved.

Okay, here it is: I first heard about it from my wife, about midnight, I think, when she heard the first report on TV, during Carson, I guess (along with Snyder, Lennon's favorite TV show). I was in the second year of writing my magnum opus about rock 'n' roll culture. I felt that in writing about rock 'n' roll and its implications throughout American culture I was really trying to come to grips with the whole meaning of my life, and I was at the end of my rope, fully extended, reaching and overreaching. And I was there because of the Beatles. Period.

Now that it's over, I'm glad I was. For a time, I was forced to find my limits and my possibilities, to become fully who I am. Because of the Beatles. We stayed up all night, I and the misty-eyed wife, and I canceled an interview the next morning with the borough president of Queens (yes, for the rock book—don't ask. . . .), and I called Kevin and talked to Mom and stayed up all day and tried to grasp the enormity of this event thrown on top of the enormity of the events that had made up John Lennon's life. Empty, empty, hollow, sick, jumping out of my skin. Turn around, go back, no, no, no. Oh, God. What now? Where? How? Even cynical Kevin was crushed. Bob, that's our *life!* The front page of the *New York Times* for December 9, 1980 read:

"JOHN LENNON OF BEATLES IS KILLED;
SUSPECT HELD IN SHOOTING AT DAKOTA

"John Lennon, one of the four Beatles, was shot and killed last night entering the apartment building where he lived, the Dakota, on Manhattan's Upper West Side. A suspect was seized at the scene.

"The 40-year-old Mr. Lennon was shot in the back twice after getting out of a limousine and walking into an entrance way of the Dakota at 1 West 72nd Street, Sgt. Robert Barnes of the 20th Precinct said."

Fuck you.

21

EPILOGUE

The Future as Epitaph

ap-Tap-Clatter-Clatter-Clatter...

The rock 'n' roll teletype is spewing copy again, even as I write. There's always another. And another. And another. That's the nature of life, I suppose. But so young? Maybe that's the nature of life *today*. Maybe rock 'n' roll stands in while war is out taking a piss. What is it that Michael Herr said in *Dispatches*? "The war primed you for lame years while rock and roll turned more lurid and dangerous than bullfighting, rock stars started falling like second lieutenants."

Tap-Tap-Clatter-Clatter-Clatter...

Who is it this time?

Riiiiip!

Los Angeles, April 1, 1984—"Marvin Gaye, who blended the soul music of the urban scene with the beat of the oldtime gospel singer and became an influential force in pop music, was shot to death today.

"The singer, who would have been forty-five years old Monday, died at 1:01 P.M. from bullet wounds in his chest at the California Hospital Medical Center. Police said they would charge his father, Marvin Gaye, Sr., seventy, with murder or manslaughter."

Oh, weep and wail! Marvin, Marvin, Marvin. "I Heard It Through the Grapevine." "Sexual Healing." "What's Going On?" Marvin, Marvin, dear sweet, beautiful, cool Marvin...

Tap-Tap-Clatter-Clatter-Clatter...

More?

Riiiiip!

Los Angeles (is *that* why it's the "City of Angels"?), May 16, 1984—"Andy Kaufman, the 'conceptual comedian' who played the wacky Latka on TV's 'Taxi' died Wednesday of lung cancer. Kaufman, thirty-six, had never smoked, according to his publicist...."

Not *Andy!* Oh my God, not Andy. Andy didn't do drugs. Andy didn't drive fast. Andy didn't even smoke! Look, it says it right here: Andy didn't even fucking smoke. Sweet, hilarious Andy...

Tap-Tap-Clatter-Clatter-Clatter...

Yeah, I know. Another.

Riiiiip!

Dennis Wilson got drunk and jumped off his boat and hit his head. Dennis Wilson was young. Dennis Wilson was crazy, being treated for it, etc.

Always the *Tap-Tap-Clatter-Clatter-Clatter.* Indeed, by the time you read this book, the *Tap-Tap* will have tolled again. I'd bet on it. Maybe more than once, maybe more than twice. A generation is killing itself because it's having trouble getting older—just as it used to kill itself because it had trouble being young. One thing I know that I didn't know so well when I started: Drugs really can kill you—you can handle 'em until you can't, as the man said—and there's not a shred of glory lying there on the stainless-steel slab waiting for a guy to peel your skin back from your forehead and put your brains in a plastic bag. Jimi Hendrix, Janis, Johnny Ace, Brian Jones: Once they were joy; now they smell up plastic garbage bags. Is that a life?

A complete rock 'n' roll call up yonder. Death's Greatest Hits. R.I.P. it up.

Who, when, and how.

Johnny Ace
1/29/29–12/24/54
Gunshot, self-inflicted

Duane Allman
11/20/46–10/29/71
Motorcycle accident

Florence Ballard (Supremes)
1/30/43–2/22/76
Heart attack

John Belushi
1/24/49–3/5/82
Cocaine and heroin

"Big Bopper"
(J. P. Richardson)
10/24/30–2/3/59
Airplane accident

Bill Black (Elvis Presley band)
9/17/26–10/21/65
Brain tumor

David Blue
2/18/41–12/2/82
Heart attack while jogging

Marc Bolan
9/30/47–9/16/77
Automobile accident

Tommy Bolin
1951–12/4/76
Heroin

John Bonham
5/31/48–9/25/80
Vodka

Tim Buckley
2/14/47–6/29/75
Heroin, suspected dosing

Dorsey Burnette
(Rock 'n' Roll Trio)
12/28/32–8/19/79
Heart attack

Johnny Burnette
(Rock 'n' Roll Trio)
3/25/34–8/1/64
Boat accident

Karen Carpenter
3/2/50–2/4/83
Starvation

Harry Chapin
12/7/42–7/16/81
Automobile accident

Eddie Cochran
10/3/38–4/17/60
Automobile accident

Sam Cooke
1/22/35–12/11/64
Gunshot

Jim Croce
1/10/43–9/20/73
Plane crash

Bobby Darin
5/14/36–12/20/73
Heart attack

Sandy Denny
1/6/41–4/21/78
Stairs

Mama Cass Elliot
9/19/43–7/29/74
Ham sandwich

Bobby Fuller
10/22/43–7/18/66
Drugs suspected

Marvin Gaye
4/2/39–4/1/84
Gunshot

Keith Godchaux
7/14/48–7/23/80
Automobile accident

Pete Ham (Badfinger)
4/27/47–4/23/75
Suicide by hanging

Tim Hardin
12/23/41–12/29/80
Heroin

Donnie Hathaway
10/1/45–1/13/79
Suicide

Jimi Hendrix
11/27/42–9/18/70
Barbiturates

Bob "Bear" Hite (Canned Heat)
2/26/45–4/5/81
Heart attack

Buddy Holly
9/7/38–2/3/59
Airplane accident

James Honeyman-Scott
(Pretenders)
11/4/57–6/16/82
Cocaine suspected

Johnny Horton ("Battle of New
Orleans")
4/30/27–11/5/60
Automobile accident

Al Jackson (Booker T.
and the MGs)
11/27/35–10/1/75
Gunshot

Brian Jones
2/28/42–7/3/69
Drowning

Janis Joplin
1/19/43–10/4/70
Heroin

Terry Kath
1/31/46–1/23/78
Gunshot, accidentally
self-inflicted

King Curtis
2/7/34–8/13/71
Gunshot

Paul Kossoff
9/14/50–3/19/76
Heart attack suspected

John Lennon
10/9/40–12/8/80
Gunshot

Frankie Lymon
9/30/42–2/28/68
Heroin

Bob Marley
2/6/45–5/9/81
Brain cancer

Van McCoy
1/6/44–7/6/79
Heart attack

Jimmy McCulloch
8/13/53–9/28/79
Heroin suspected

Robbie McIntosh
(Average White Band)
1950–9/23/74
Heroin, dosed

Ron "Pigpen" McKernan
9/8/45–3/8/73
Cirrhosis

Clyde McPhatter
11/15/33–6/13/72
Heart, liver, kidney disease

Keith Moon
8/23/47–9/7/78
Barbiturates

Jim Morrison
12/8/43–7/3/71
Heroin suspected (officially,
heart attack)

Berry Oakley
4/4/48–11/11/72
Motorcycle accident

Phil Ochs
12/19/40–4/9/76
Suicide by hanging

Felix Pappalardi
1939–4/17/83
Gunshot

Junior Parker
3/3/27–11/18/71
Brain surgery

Gram Parsons
11/5/46–9/19/73
Drugs

Elvis Presley
1/8/35–8/16/77
Heart attack, drugs suspected

Otis Redding
9/9/41–12/10/67
Airplane crash

Keith Relf (Yardbirds)
3/22/43–5/14/76
Electrocution

Minnie Riperton
11/8/47–7/12/79
Cancer

Bon Scott (AC/DC)
7/9/46–2/19/80
Alcohol, possible drugs

Joe Tex
8/9/33–8/13/82
Heart attack

Ritchie Valens
5/13/41–2/3/59
Airplane crash

Gene Vincent
2/11/43–10/12/71
Ulcer

Clarence White (Byrds)
6/6/44–7/73
Struck by automobile

Hank Williams
9/17/23–1/1/53
Drugs

Paul Williams (Temptatons)
9/19/40–8/17/73
Gunshot, self-inflicted

Chuck Willis ("C. C. Rider")
1/31/28–4/10/58
Ulcer

Alan Wilson (Canned Heat)
7/4/43–9/3/70
Barbiturates

Chris Wood (Traffic)
6/24/44–7/12/83
Cancer

SOURCE NOTES

CHAPTER 2—HANK WILLIAMS

5 *"A poet..."* Greil Marcus, *Mystery Train* (New York: Dutton, 1975), p. 151.

5 *"As I walked..."* Hank Williams, Jr., *Living Proof* (co-written with Michael Bane) (New York: G.P. Putnam's Sons, 1970), p.65.

6 *"[Hank] provided a prototype..."* Michael Bane, *The Outlaws: Revolution in Country Music* (New York: Country Music Magazine Press/Doubleday/Dolphin, 1978), p. 19.

7 *"Tee-Tot taught..."* Living Proof, p.58.

8 *"Imagine Elvis..."* Ibid., p. 61.

8 *"There were demons..."* Ibid., p.61.

9 *"Daddy had hired..."* Ibid., p. 63.

10 *"They came to Montgomery..."* Ibid., p. 9.

CHAPTER 4—BUDDY HOLLY

17 *"He was a quiet kid..."* Buddy Holly chapter by Jonathan Cott, *Rolling Stone Illustrated History of Rock & Roll*, ed. by Jim Miller (New York: Rolling Stone Press/Random House, 1976), p. 78.

CHAPTER 5—SAM COOKE

21 *"Thousands of screaming..."* *Chicago Defender*, Dec. 14, 1964, as reprinted in *Rolling Stone Illustrated History of Rock & Roll*, p. 114.

23 *"whose quivering tenor..."* Joe McEwen in *The Rolling Stone Illustrated History of Rock & Roll*, p. 114.

24 *"Sam Cooke became..."* Phllip Norman, *Shout! The Beatles in their Generation* (New York: Warner Books, 1981), p. 442.

24 *"From that point on..."* Joe McEwen in *The Rolling Stone Illustrated History of Rock & Roll*, p. 116.

CHAPTER 6—OTIS REDDING

27 *"My original feeling..."* Lenny Kaye and David Dalton, *Rock 100* (New York: Grosset & Dunlap, 1977), p. 138.

29 *"He was a shy..."* *Chicago Daily News*, Dec. 17, 1967.

Chapter 7—Brian Jones

33   *"After we had split up . . ."* Mandy Aftel, *Death of a Rolling Stone: The Brian Jones Story* (New York: Delilah Books, 1982), p. 108.

35   *"Brian was the first . . ."* Ibid., p. 37.

35   *"In the early sixties . . ."* Tony Sanchez, *Up and Down with the Rolling Stones* (New York: Signet/New American Library, 1979), p. 12.

36   *"We knew all along . . ."* Ibid., p. 13.

36   *"Brian was still loving it . . ."* Ibid., p. 21

36   *"She had only to walk . . ."* Ibid., p. 21

36   *"Brian threw himself . . ."* *Death of a Rolling Stone*, p. 121.

37   *"As a couple . . ."* *Up and Down with the Rolling Stones*, p. 23.

37   *"What I firmly believe . . ."* BBC radio transcript as printed in *Death of a Rolling Stone*, p. 144.

38   *"marked the peak . . ."* *Up and Down with the Rolling Stones*, p. 23.

38   *"Seems like you . . ."* Ibid., p. 27

38   *"After about the third year . . ."* *Death of a Rolling Stone*, p. 128.

38   *"Everybody felt . . ."* Ibid., p. 142.

39   *"We arranged . . ."* Ibid., p. 143.

39   *"He searched the room . . ."* Ibid., p. 143.

40   *"He had this incredible . . ."* Ibid., p. 150.

40   *"I understand now . . ."* *Up and Down with the Rolling Stones*, p. 81.

41   *"He vacillates . . ."* *Death of a Rolling Stone*, p. 164.

41   *"He celebrated his release . . ."* *Up and Down with the Rolling Stones*, p. 81.

42   *"I'm going to kill . . ."* Ibid., p. 114.

42   *"pathetic"* *Death of a Rolling Stone*, p. 186.

43   *"His heart was . . ."* Ibid., p. 202.

43   *"immersion in fresh water . . ."* *Up and Down with the Rolling Stones*, p. 166.

Chapter 8—Jimi Hendrix

47   *"I was talking . . ."* Jerry Hopkins, *Hit and Run: The Jimi Hendrix Story* (New York: Perigee/Putnam, 1983), p. 35.

47   *"We liked that cough syrup . . ."* Ibid., p. 35.

48   *"magnetic . . ."* Curtis Knight, *Jimi: An Intimate Biography*, as reprinted in *Hit and Run*, p. 73.

48   *"He liked it a lot . . ."* Ibid., p. 75.

48   *"She really dug him . . ."* *Hit and Run*, p. 73.

48   *"I was the hot-shot . . ."* Donn Menn ed., "Johnny Winter Reminisces," *Guitar Player*, September 1975, p. 16.

49   *"the new guitar in town . . ."* *Hit and Run*, p. 97.

50   *"At first he . . ."* Ibid., p. 129.

50   *"Eric Burdon was on . . ."* Ibid., p. 134.

50   *"He had started drinking . . ."* David Henderson, *'Scuse Me While I Kiss the Sky: The Life of Jimi Hendrix* (New York: Bantam, 1983), p. 169.

51   *"Are there . . . uh . . ."* *Hit and Run*, p. 151.

51   *"We needed a ratio . . ."* Ibid., p. 153.

52   *"Screw 'im . . ."* Ibid., p. 184.

53   *"Jimi was visibly..."* Ibid., p. 216.
53   *"Hurry! I need help..."* Ibid., p. 222.
54   *"Lemme think..."* Ibid., p. 227.
55   *"In those days..."* Ibid., p. 257.
55   *"When I saw him..."* "Johnny Winter Reminisces," p. 13.
57   *"He was consuming drugs..."* Hit and Run, p. 286.
57   *"I've been dead..."* Hit and Run, p. 291.
57   *"I don't want..."* Rolling Stone, November 15,1969, as reprinted in *Hit and Run*, p. 244.
57   *"He didn't seem like his..."* Ibid., p. 297.
58   *"Remember this..."* Ibid., p. 300.
58   *"When we came back..."* Ibid., p. 301
58   *"a result of inhalation..."* Ibid., p. 309.
58   *"made his exit..."* Ibid., p. 305.

CHAPTER 9—JIM MORRISON

59   *"I don't know how many times..."* Jerry Hopkins and Danny Sugarman, *No One Here Gets Out Alive* (New York: Warner Books, 1980), p. 21.
61   *"Your father's a..."* Ibid., p. 40.
62   *"Those are the greatest..."* Ibid., p. 61.
62   *"posing in front..."* Ibid., p. 75.
63   *"I never took..."* Ibid., p. 93.
64   *"You could say it's..."* Press kit from Elektra Records, as reprinted in *No One Here Gets Out Alive*, p. 106.
65   *"unendurable pleasure..."* Review by Lillian Roxon (publishing information unavailable) as reprinted in *No One Here Gets Out Alive*, p. 121.
66   *"One thing, Jim..."* No One Here Gets Out Alive, p. 136.
67   *"wanted some privacy..."* and other onstage remarks, Ibid., p. 162.
68   *"buttfucking..."* Ibid., p. 166.
68   *"Let's face it..."* Ibid., p. 175.
70   *"a bunch of slaves..."* Ibid., p. 231
71   *"lewd and lascivious..."* Ibid., p. 236.
72   *"He looked waxen..."* Ibid., p. 417.
72   *"Does anyone believe in..."* Ibid., p. 313.
73   *"You're drinking with..."* Ibid., p. 314.
73   *"If I had it to do..."* Circus magazine, as reprinted in *No One Here Gets Out Alive*, p. 317.
73   *"He lost all his..."* No One Here Gets Out Alive, p. 330.
75   *"I know people drink..."* L.A. Free Press, as reprinted in *No One Here Gets Out Alive*, p. 339.

CHAPTER 10—JANIS JOPLIN

78   *"far beyond anything..."* Myra Friedman, *Buried Alive: The Biography of Janis Joplin* (New York: William Morrow & Company, 1973), p. 17.
79   *"Janis was publicity..."* Ibid., p. 42.

79   *"I wanted to smoke..."* David Dalton, *Janis Joplin* (New York: Simon & Schuster, 1971), p. 36.

80   *"Don't let anybody..."* Buried Alive, p. 54.

80   *"a vegetable..."* Ibid., p.58.

81   *"They wanted to see... "* Rolling Stone, as reprinted in *Janis Joplin*, p.239.

82   *"attained acceptance..."* Buried Alive, p. 94.

84   Excerpts from *Going Down with Janis*, Peggy Caserta, *Going Down with Janis* (New York: Lyle Stuart, 1973), pp. 7, 9, 102, 181.

87   *"This is Janis..."* Buried Alive, p. 126.

87   *"She was always talking..."* Ibid., p. 196.

88   *"Well, I have to go..."* Ibid., p. 179.

88   *"They called her..."* Ibid., p. 298.

89   *"Oh, I dunno..."* Ibid., p. 324.

CHAPTER 11—GRAM PARSONS

91   *"I couldn't wait..."* Eve Babitz, *Rolling Stone*, October 25, 1973.

93   *"When he runs out..."* Judith Sims, *Rolling Stone,* March 1, 1973.

93   *"the kind of place..."* Patrick Sullivan, *Rolling Stone*, October 25, 1973.

94   *"What department?..."* Eve Babitz, *Rolling Stone*, October 25, 1973.

94   *"I just passed..."* Judith Sims, *Rolling Stone*, March 1, 1973.

95   *"I started going out there..."* Ibid.

97   *"I wanted to take..."* Ibid.

97   *"His hands were..."* Eve Babitz, *Rolling Stone*, October 25, 1973.

98   *"He had split..."* Patrick Sullivan, *Rolling Stone*, October 25, 1973.

98   *"He was always anxious..."* Ibid.

99   *"It was Gram's request..."* Ibid.

CHAPTER 12—DUANE ALLMAN AND BERRY OAKLEY

101   *"Gregg and Duane Allman..."* Glover Lewis, *Rolling Stone*, November 25, 1971.

102   *"Red Dog remarks..."* Ibid.

103   *"Duane and Dickey lope..."* Ibid.

103   *"I'm not gonna do..."* Ibid.

CHAPTER 14—SID VICIOUS

113   *"If anyone overestimated..."* Julie Burchill and Tony Parsons, *The Boy Looked at Johnny: The Obituary of Rock and Roll* (London: The Pluto Press, 1978), p. 42.

114   *"All you cowboys..."* Patrick Goldstein, *Creem*, April 1978.

114   *"root of all..."* The Boy Looked at Johnny, p. 42.

115   *"As the band prepared..."* Ibid., p. 43.

115   *"Malcolm was setting me..."* Susan Whitall, *Creem,* April 1978.

CHAPTER 15—KEITH MOON

120   *"I'm going to throw. . . ."* Dave Marsh, *Before I Get Old: The Story of the Who*
       (New York: St. Martin's Press, 1983), p. 475.
120   *"I tried to open it . . ."* Ibid., p. 475.
121   *"as soon as Keith came in contact. . . ."* Ibid., p. 81.
121   *"Dyed ginger hair. . . ."* Ibid., p. 79
121   *"When Keith joined. . . ."* Ibid., p. 88.
121   *"Moon was incredible . . . ."* Ibid., p. 149.
122   *"Moon did his usual. . . ."* Ibid., p. 201.
122   *"When the festival ended. . . ."* Ibid., p. 259.
122   *"That's how I lost. . . ."* Steve Clarke, *The Who in Their Own Words* (New
       York: Delilah Books, 1979), p. 85.
123   *"I get bored. . . ."* Ibid., p. 92.
124   *"We were smashing. . . ."* Ibid., p. 102.
124   *"Six weeks later. . . ."* Ibid., p. 102.
124   *"Nevertheless, Keith sank. . . ."* *Before I Get Old.*
125   The description of dinner at chez Moon. Dougal Butler, *Full Moon: The
       Amazing Rock & Roll Life of Keith Moon* (New York: William Morrow &
       Company, 1981), p. 174.
125   *"My way of life . . ."* *The Who In Their Own Words,* p. 91.
125   *"Moonie's room is . . ."* Ibid., p. 31.
126   *"Keith stumbled through. . . ."* *Before I Get Old,* p. 413.
127   *"The conclusion of the album. . . ."* Ibid., p. 414.
127   *"Moonie played games. . . ."* Ibid., p. 494.
128   *"I feel I've got a sense. . . ."* *Rolling Stone,* as reprinted in *Before I Get Old,*

CHAPTER 16—JOHN BELUSHI

131   *"That's what I. . . ."* Bob Woodward, *Wired: The Short Life and Fast Times of
       John Belushi* (New York: Simon & Schuster, 1984), p. 37.
131   *"He's the most. . . ."* Ibid., p. 37.
132   *"We all have our personal. . . ."* *Chicago Daily News,* April 15, 1972.
132   That there was a lot of cocaine, and other drug information here, was gleaned
       from *Wired.*
132   *"One day John would. . . ."* *Wired,* p. 103.
133   *"Smokes 3 packs. . . ."* Ibid., p. 103.
133   *"I give so much. . . ."* Ibid., p. 105.
133   *"What you have to remember. . . ."* Mitch Glazer, *Crawdaddy,* June 1977.
134   *"explaining to Judy. . . ."* *Wired,* p. 111.
134   *"(Lorne) Michaels thought it was. . . ."* *Wired,* p. 132.
135   *"One week, during his. . . ."* Lorne Michaels, *Rolling Stone,* April 29, 1982.
136   *"There sat Belushi. . . ."* *Wired,* p. 20.
137   *"John was. . .blowing. . . ."* Ibid., p. 301.
137   *"Bear had a lot. . . ."* Ibid., p. 344.

138   *"I have a lot of friends..."* Ibid., p. 269.
138   *"Have you ever..."* Ibid., p. 283.
138   *"People, the man..."* Dan Aykroyd, *Rolling Stone,* April 29, 1982.
139   *"He sounded like a..."* Wired, p. 346.
139   *"Hey, I like..."* Ibid., p. 363.
140   *"John stood up..."* Ibid., p. 398.
140   *"trashy..."* Ibid., p. 399.
140   *"You haven't had any...."* and other quotes from Belushi's final hours, Ibid.,
           pp. 399, 400.
141   *"John Belushi, a 33-year-old..."* Ibid., p. 414.

Chapter 17—Bob Marley

144   *"on Marcus Garvey Drive..."* Timothy White, *Catch a Fire: The Life of Bob
           Marley* (New York: Holt, Rinehart and Winston, 1983) p. 143.
145   *"Bob had composed..."* Ibid., p. 158.
145   *"Reaction in the gutter..."* Ibid., p. 159.
147   *"Blackwell had heard..."* Ibid., p. 233.
148   *"drawing on a spliff..."* Ibid., p. 261.
148   *"The American press..."* Ibid., p. 261.
149   *"Bob was in the kitchen..."* Ibid., p. 288.
150   *"The gunman got off..."* Ibid., p. 289.
151   *"The last thing they..."* Ibid., p. 292.
152   *"Me gwan die..."* Ibid., p. 298.
152   *"Doctor seh..."* Ibid., p. 309.
153   *"Issels managed..."* Ibid., p. 312.
153   *"Maddah, don't cry..."* Ibid., p. 313.

Chapter 18—Karen Carpenter

156   *"Karen had been a little overweight..."* Richard Carpenter as told to Suzanne
           Adelson, *People,* November 21, 1983.
156   *"At a back table..."* Tom Nolan, *Rolling Stone,* July 4, 1974.
157   *"That year..."* People.
157   *"This DJ from Toronto..."* Rolling Stone.
157   *"Boy there've been..."* Ibid.
157   *"From early 1975..."* Ibid.

Chapter 19—Elvis Presley

161   *"Elvis ... transcends his talent..."* Greil Marcus, *Mystery Train: Images of
           America in Rock 'n' Roll Music* (New York: E.P. Dutton, 1975), p. 138.
162   *"I was the hero..."* Albert Goldman, *Elvis* (New York: McGraw-Hill, 1981),
           p. 129.
163   *"What [Elvis] sought..."* Ibid., p. 338.

163   *"When he took over..."* Red West, Sonny West, Dave Hebler, as told to Steve Dunleavy, *Elvis: What Happened?* (New York: Ballantine Books, 1977), p. 279.

163   *"Elvis likes to boast..."* Elvis, p. 23.

164   *"Dave Hebler remembers..."* Elvis, p. 311.

165   *"Elvis doesn't like..."* Ibid., p. 80.

165   *"He firmly believes..."* Ibid., p. 157.

165   *"He used to return..."* Ibid., p. 159.

166   *"The man [Elvis] is repeating..."* Ibid., p. 4.

166   *"[Elvis] took that pool cue..."* Ibid., p. 30.

166   *"[Elvis] takes pills..."* Ibid., p. 286.

167   *"Elvis changed into..."* Elvis, p. 562.

167   *"GIRL ELVIS WAS..."* Ginger Alden, *National Enquirer*, September 6, 1977.

168   *"I'm not fucked..."* Elvis, p. 328.

CHAPTER 21—EPILOGUE

173   *"Marvin Gaye..."* New York Times, April 2, 1984.

175   *"Andy Kaufman, the 'conceptual comedian'..."* San Francisco Chronicle, May 17, 1984.

INDEX

Ace, Johnny, 11–15
Aftel, Mandy, 38, 39
"Alabama," 108
Alden, Ginger, 167–68
Alexander, J. W., 23–24, 25
"All Along the Watchtower," 52
Allison, Jerry, 18–19
Allman Brothers Band, 101–5, 107, 109
Allman Brothers Band at Fillmore East, The, 102
Allman, Duane, 101–5 107, 110
Allman, Gregg, 101, 102
"Anarchy in the U.K.," 113
Andrew, Sam, 84
Animals, 48–49
"Another Saturday Night," 24
Axis: Bold as Love, 50, 51
Aykroyd, Dan, 132, 135, 136, 138–39, 140

Babitz, Eve, 97
"Back Door Man," 67
Band of Gypsies, 54–55
Bane, Michael, 6
Bar-Kays, 31, 32
Barrett, Aston and Carlton, 146–47

Beatles, 8, 23, 24, 30, 69, 84, 104, 145, 148, 169–72
Beggars' Banquet, 41–42
"Belsen Was a Gas," 115
Belushi, Adam, 131
Belushi, John, 97, 129–41
Belushi, Judy Jacklin, 131, 132, 133–34, 136, 139, 140
Betts, Dickey, 101, 102
Big Bopper (J. P. Richardson), 19, 20
Big Brother and the Holding Company, 81, 82–83, 84, 88
Blackwell, Chris, 147, 148
Blackwell, Robert "Bumps," 23–24
Bland, Bobby "Blue," 11
Bloomfield, Mike, 48, 49, 87
"Blowin' in the Wind," 23
Blues Brothers, 135, 136
Blues Brothers, The, 137
Blues Magoos, 122
Boland, Neil, 124
Boyer, Lisa, 25–26
"Break on Through," 64, 65
Briefcase Full of Blues, 135
"Bring It on Home to Me," 24
Brown, James, 29, 30, 31
Buddy Holly Story, The, 128

Burchill, Julie, 113, 115
Burdon, Eric, 45, 50, 58
Burnin', 148
Burns, Bob, 108, 110
Burrito Deluxe, 97
Butler, Dougal, 125–26
Byrds, 95, 96

Carpenter, Karen, 155–58
Carpenter, Richard, 156–57
Carr, Charles, 9
Caserta, Peggy, 84–86, 89
Catch a Fire, 147–48
Cauley, Ben, 32
"Chain Gang," 24
Chandler, Chas, 48–49, 50, 51, 54
"Change Is Gonna Come, A," 24
"Chantilly Lace," 19
Charles, Ray, 30, 138
Chase, Chevy, 132
Cheap Thrills, 83, 84
Clapton, Eric, 42, 104, 148
Cliff, Jimmy, 144
"C'mon Let's Go," 19
"Cold Cold Heart," 8
Collins, Allen, 108, 110
"Concrete Jungle," 148
Continental Divide, 137
Cooke, Sam, 21–26, 27, 29, 31
Coon Dog, 93
Country Joe and the Fish, 82
Courson, Pamela, 68, 72, 74
Cox, Billy, 47, 54, 57
Crickets, 18–19
Cropper, Steve, 27–29
Crosby, David, 49
"Cupid," 24
Curbishley, Bill and Jackie, 120
Curtis, Sonny, 19

Dalton, David, 29, 79
Danneman, Monika, 57–58
Davis, Clive, 83

"Day Tripper," 30
DeNiro, Robert, 140
Densmore, John, 62, 63–64, 68
Detours, 121
Dixon, Deborah, 38
"Dock of the Bay," 27, 31, 32
Doors, 62–75, 86
Douglas, Alan, 53
Drifting Cowboys, 7
Dylan, Bob, 11, 17, 23, 24, 48, 52,
    68, 82

Eagles, 10
Electric Ladyland, 52
"End, The," 1, 64
Entwistle, John, 121
Erikson, Roky, 80
Ethridge, Chris, 96
Exile on Main Street, 96

Faithful, Marianne, 42, 49
Feast of Friends, 69
First Rays of the New Rising Sun, 56
Flying Burrito Brothers, 96, 97, 98
Franklin, Aretha, 30, 31, 104
Franklin, Bertha, 26
"Freebird," 107, 108
Friedman, Myra, 78–79, 80, 82,
    83–84, 87, 88–89, 90
Full Tilt Boogie, 87–88

Gaines, Cassie, 110
Gaines, Steven, 110
Gaye, Marvin, 173–75
Gaye, Marvin, Sr., 173
"Get Up, Stand Up," 148
Gilded Palace of Sin, The, 96
Going Down with Janis, 84–86
Goin' South, 134
Goldman, Albert, 161, 163–64, 167
GP, 97, 98
Grand Ole Opry, 8, 9
Grateful Dead, 82, 102

Gravenites, Nick, 87
Green, Dr., 40, 41
Grossman, Albert, 82, 83, 86
Guess, Don, 19

Hammond, John, Jr., 48
"Happy Jack," 119
Hard Day's Night, 84
Harris, R. H., 23
Harrison, George, 40
"Having a Party," 24
Hazelwood, Lee, 94
"Hello, I Love You," 69
Helms, Chet, 79, 80–81, 88
Henderson, David, 50–51
Hendrix, Al, 45–47, 51
Hendrix, Jimi, 31, 40, 45–58, 72,
    89, 102, 129–31
Hendrix, Leon, 47
Hendrix, Lucille, 45–47, 51
Herman's Hermits, 122
"Hey, Good Lookin'," 8
"Hey Jude," 104
Hillman, Chris, 96
Hollies, 17
Holly, Buddy, 2, 17–20, 36, 128
Holly, Maria Elena, 19
"Honky Tonkin'," 8
Hopkins, Jerry, 53, 64, 71, 72, 74
"Hound Dog," 159
HWY, 71

"I Can See for Miles," 122
"I Can't Explain," 121
"I'll Never Get Out of This World
    Alive," 10
"In Memory of Elizabeth Reed," 101
International Submarine Band, 94
"I Saw the Light," 5
"I Shot the Sheriff," 148
"I've Been Loving You Too Long,'
    27

Jacklin, Judy, 131, 132, 133–34,
    136, 139, 140
Jagger, Mick, 27, 33, 35, 36, 38, 40,
    42–43, 44, 49, 95, 97
"Jailhouse Rock," 159
"Jambalaya," 8, 9
Jefferson Airplane, 82
Jeffery, Mike, 54, 57
Jennings, Waylon, 19
Jimi at Berkeley, 56
Jimi Hendrix Experience, 50, 52, 55
Jimmy James and the Blue Flames,
    48
Johnny Jenkins and the Pinetoppers,
    29, 30
Johns, Glyn, 127
Jones, Brian, 17, 33–44, 49, 53, 109
Jones, Lewis, 35, 37
Jones, Louise, 35
Joplin, Janis, 31, 66, 68, 73, 77–90,
    104, 122, 129
"Judge Not," 144
"Jumpin' Jack Flash," 35

Karpen, Julius, 81, 82
Kaufman, Andy, 175
Kaufman, Phil, 98, 99
"Kaw-Liga," 8
Kaye, Lenny, 29
King, B. B., 11
King, Ed, 108, 110
Klein, Allen, 24
Kleinow, "Sneeky" Peter, 96
Knight, Curtis, 47, 48
Kong, Leslie, 144
Kooper, Al, 108
Korner, Alexis, 35
Kozmic Blues Band, 86
Krieger, Robby, 62, 68
Kristofferson, Kris, 87

Landau, Jon, 29, 32
Landis, John, 36

L.A. Woman, 73
Lawrence, Linda, 33, 37
Lawson, Janet, 43
Layla, 104
Leibovitz, Annie, 103
Lennon, John, 42, 161, 169–72
"Light My Fire," 65
"Little Red Rooster," 24
Little Richard, 29, 30, 47
Livingston, Bunny, 144, 146, 151
Lords, The, 71, 74
"Lovable," 23–24
"Love Me Tender," 159
"Love Reign O'er Me," 127
"Lover Man," 53
"Lovesick Blues," 8
Lynyrd Skynyrd, 102, 107–10

McCartney, Paul, 17, 49, 128
McDonald, Country Joe, 81
McEwen, Joe, 23, 24
McGuinn, Roger, 95
McLaren, Malcom, 111, 114, 115
Manley, Michael, 149, 150–51
Manzarek, Ray, 61, 62, 63–64, 68, 69, 70, 73
Marcus, Greil, 5, 8, 161
Marley, Bob, 143–53
Marley, Cedella, 143–44, 145, 153
Marley, Norval Sinclair, 143
Marley, Rita, 146, 150, 152
Marsh, Dave, 122, 124, 126–27
Marshall Tucker Band, 102
Martin, Michael, 98, 99
Matlock, Glen, 113
"Mercedes Benz," 77
Michaels, Lorne, 132, 134, 135–36
Miles, Buddy, 49, 54–55
Mitchell, Mitch, 52
Monterey Pop, 40, 49
Monterey Pop Festival, 31, 40, 49, 82, 122
Moon, Alfred, 120

Moon, Keith, 119–28, 129
Moon, Kim, 124–25
Moon, Kitty, 120–21
Moon, Mandy, 125
"Moonlight Drive," 62
Morgan, Seth, 89
Morrison, Andy, 59, 65
Morrison, Clara, 61, 65–66, 71
Morrison, George, 61, 65, 66, 71
Morrison, Jerry, 53–54
Morrison, Jim, 1–2, 10, 17, 59–75, 83, 86, 104, 109
Morrison, Pamela Courson, 68, 72, 74
Morrison Hotel, 73
"Music Must Change," 128
"My Lover's Prayer," 27
"My Song," 11

Nash, Johnny, 147
National Lampoon's Animal House, 134, 135, 136
Neighbors, 137
Neuwirth, Bobby, 68, 87
Never Mind the Bollocks, Here's the Sex Pistols, 113
Nevison, Ron, 127
New Creatures, The, 71, 74
Nicholson, Jack, 134
1941, 135, 137
Noguchi, Thomas, 90
Nolan, Tom, 156
No One Here Gets Out Alive, 64
Norman, Phillip, 24
"Not Fade Away," 36
Notorious Byrd Brothers, The, 95

Oakley, Berry, 101–5
Oakley, Linda, 105
O'Donoghue, Michael, 133
One Love Peace Festival, 151
Ono, Yoko, 42

Pallenberg, Anita, 36–39, 40
Parsons, Gram, 91–99
Parsons, Robert, 93, 99
Parsons, Tony, 113, 115
Payne, Rufus "Tee-Tot," 7
Pearl, 88, 89
Pearl, Minnie, 5–6
Pearson, Ken, 89
"Peggy Sue," 18
Performance, 36
Perry, Lee "Scratch," 146–47
Petty, Norman, 19
Pickett, Wilson, 104
Plaster Casters, 51–52, 53
"Pledging My Love," 13
Pollard, Michael J., 87
Potier, Suki, 40
Powell, Billy, 108, 110
Presley, Elvis, 8, 18, 93, 159–68,
  169
Pronounced Leh-Nerd Skin-Nerd,
  108
Pyle, Artimus, 110

Quadrophenia, 108, 126–27

Rainbow Bridge, 56
Rawls, Lou, 24
Redding, Noel, 50, 52
Redding, Otis, 27–32, 81, 122
Red Dog, 102
"Respect," 30
Richards, Keith, 33, 35, 36, 38–39,
  40, 42–43, 95, 96, 97, 135, 138,
  156
Richardson, J. P. (the Big Bopper),
  19, 20
Ritchie, John Simon (Sid Vicious), 2,
  111–17
Rock 'n' Roll Circus, The, 42
Rodgers, Jimmie, 18
Rolling Stones, 24, 30, 33–44, 48,
  95, 96, 124, 148

Rose, Fred and Wesley, 8
Rossington, Gary, 108, 110
Rotten, Johnny, 113–14, 115, 116
Roxon, Lillian, 65, 90

Safe at Home, 94
Sanchez, Tony, 35, 36–37, 38, 41
Santiago, Maria Elena, 19
"Satisfaction," 27, 30
"Saturday Night," 132, 133, 134,
  135, 136
Scoppa, Bud, 97
Second City, 132
Second Helping, 108, 109
"Seven Bridges Road," 10
Sex Pistols, 111–15
"Shake," 24
Sheppard, Audrey Mae, 7–8, 9
Shilos, 93
"Simmer Down," 145
Sinatra, Frank, 49
"Sin City" 96
"Six More Miles to the Graveyard, "
  8
Slugger (member of Ace's band),
  13–15
Smith, Cathy, 139–41
Smith, Larry "Legs," 124
Smith, Patti, 65, 116
Soul Rebels, 147
Soul Revolution, 147
Soul Stirrers, 23, 24
Spielberg, Steven, 135
Spungen, Nancy Laura, 114–16
"Statesboro Blues," 104
Stewart, Jim, 29
Stickells, Gerry, 50
Stills, Stephen, 49
"Stir It Up," 148
Street Survivors, 110
"Substitute," 121, 122
Sugarman, Danny, 64, 72, 74
Sweetheart of the Rodeo, 95

"Sweet Home Alabama," 109

"Take These Chains From My
   Heart," 10
Taylor, Don, 149–50
Taylor, Mick, 44
"Teenage Sonata," 24
"That'll Be the Day," 18, 19
"That Smell," 110
"These Arms of Mine," 27, 29
Thorogood, Frank, 43
Tommy, 124
Tork, Peter, 49
Tosh, Peter, 144, 146, 151
"Touch Me," 69
Townshend, Pete, 121, 122, 126,
   127, 128
"Try a Little Tenderness," 27
"Twistin' the Night Away," 24

Valens, Ritchie, 19, 20
Van Zant, Ronnie, 107–10
Vicious, Sid, 2, 111–17

Wailers, 144–51
Waiting for the Sun, 69
Walter-Lax, Annette, 128
Waters, Muddy, 35
Wendell, Smokey, 137, 140
West, Red, 163, 164–65, 168
Western and Pop Band, 18

Wet Willie, 102
"When the Music's Over," 62
White, Timothy, 144, 145, 147, 148,
   149–50, 151, 152
Who, The, 42, 108, 119–28
Who Are You, 127
"Wild Horses," 95
Wilkeson, Leon, 108, 110
Williams, Audrey Mae, 7–8, 9
Williams, Hank, 3–10, 18
Williams, Hank, Jr., 5, 7, 8–10
Williams, Lilly, 6–7
Williams, Lycrecia, 6, 7
Williams, Robin, 140
Wills, Bob, 18
Wilson, Dennis, 175
Wilson, Devon, 48
Winter, Johnny, 55
Wired, 129, 131, 133, 136, 137–38,
   139
"Wonderful World," 24, 27
Woodstock, 55
Woodstock Festival, 53, 54
Woodward, Bob, 129, 131, 132–33,
   134, 136, 137, 138, 139, 140
"WPA Blues, The," 7

Young, Neil, 49, 108
Young, Steve, 10
"Your Cheatin' Heart," 8
"You Send Me," 24, 27